Conversations with John Steinbeck

D0205896

Literary Conversations Series

Peggy Whitman Prenshaw
General Editor

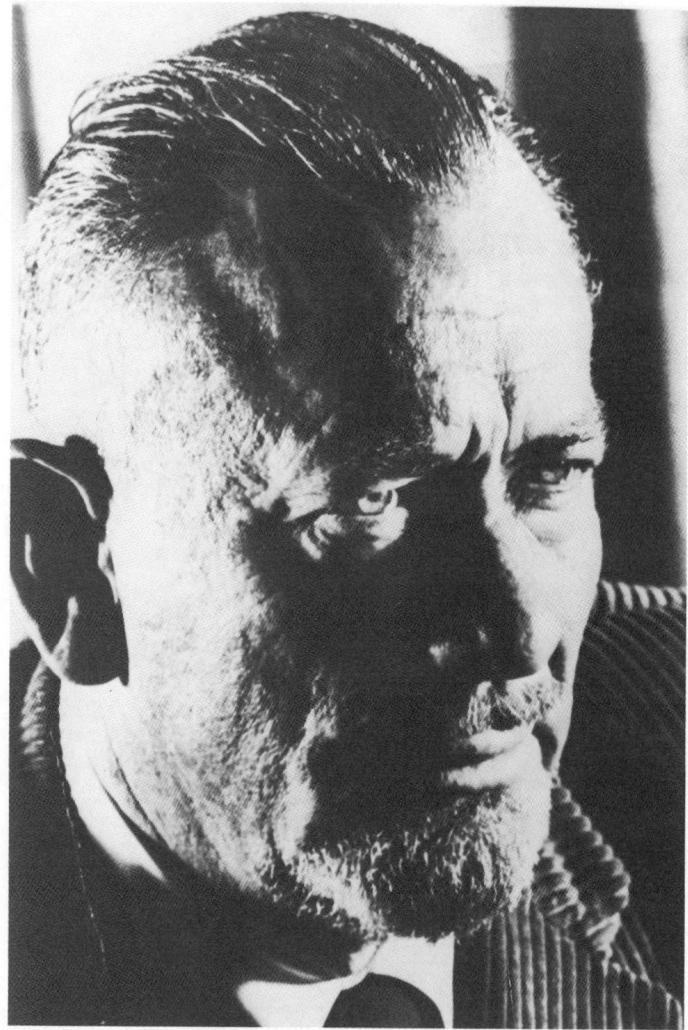
Photo: Paul Farber/Courtesy of The John Steinbeck Library, Salinas, California and Viking-Penguin, New York

Conversations with John Steinbeck

Edited by
Thomas Fensch

University Press of Mississippi
Jackson and London

Copyright © 1988 by the University Press of Mississippi
All rights reserved
91 90 89 88   4 3 2 1
The paper in this book meets the guidelines for permanence and durability of the Committee
on Production Guidelines for Book Longevity of the Council on Library Resources

Library of Congress Cataloging-in-Publication Data

Steinbeck, John, 1902-1968.
  Conversations with John Steinbeck / edited by Thomas Fensch.
      p.   cm. — (Literary conversations series)
  "Books by John Steinbeck": p.
  Includes index.
  ISBN 0-87805-359-X (alk. paper). ISBN 0-87805-360-3 (pbk. : alk.
paper)
    1. Steinbeck, John, 1902-1968—Interviews.   2. Authors,
American—20th century—Interviews.   I. Fensch, Thomas.   II. Title.
III. Series.
PS3537.T3234Z464 1988
813'.52—dc19
[B]   88-17538
                                                                                                   CIP

Books by John Steinbeck

Cup of Gold. New York: Robert M. McBride & Co., 1929.
Pastures of Heaven. New York: Brewer, Warren and Putnam, 1932.
To a God Unknown. New York: Robert O. Ballou, 1933.
Tortilla Flat. New York: Covici-Friede, 1935.
In Dubious Battle. New York: Covici-Friede, 1936.
Of Mice and Men. New York: Covici-Friede, 1937.
The Red Pony. New York: The Viking Press, 1937.
The Long Valley. New York: The Viking Press, 1938.
The Grapes of Wrath. New York: The Viking Press, 1939.
The Forgotten Village. New York: The Viking Press, 1941.
Steinbeck, John and Ricketts, Edward F. *Sea of Cortez: A Leisurely Journal of Travel
    and Research*. New York: The Viking Press, 1941.
Bombs Away: The Story of a Bomber Team. New York: The Viking Press, 1942.
The Moon Is Down. New York: The Viking Press, 1942.
Cannery Row. New York: The Viking Press, 1945.
The Wayward Bus. New York: The Viking Press, 1947.
The Pearl. New York: The Viking Press, 1947.
A Russian Journal. New York: The Viking Press, 1948.
Burning Bright. New York: The Viking Press, 1950.
The Log from the Sea of Cortez. New York: The Viking Press, 1951.
East of Eden. New York: The Viking Press, 1952.
Sweet Thursday. New York: The Viking Press, 1954.
The Short Reign of Pippin IV. New York: The Viking Press, 1957.
Once There Was a War. New York: The Viking Press, 1958.
The Winter of Our Discontent. New York: The Viking Press, 1961.
Travels with Charley in Search of America. New York: The Viking Press, 1962.
America and Americans. New York: The Viking Press, 1966.
Journal of a Novel: The East of Eden Letters. New York: The Viking Press, 1969.
The Acts of King Arthur and His Noble Knights. New York: Farrar, Straus and Giroux,
    1976.

Contents

Introduction

John Steinbeck's life, it seems in retrospect, can be seen in three phases: his California years, the war years of the early 1940s, and the years after the Second World War.

In his early years in California, in and around Monterey Bay (Salinas, Pacific Grove, Los Gatos, Monterey) he published his first three books with three different publishers: *Cup of Gold* (1929); *Pastures of Heaven* (1932) and *To a God Unknown* (1933). All three publishing firms went bankrupt during the Depression. He finally found fame and financial success with *Tortilla Flat* (1935).

The publication of *Tortilla Flat* cemented the professional and personal relationships which he kept for the rest of his career. His literary properties were sold through the McIntosh & Otis agency in New York, and he became warm friends with Mavis McIntosh, Elizabeth Otis, and others in the agency. Pascal Covici discovered him and published *Tortilla Flat* under the imprint of his firm, Covici-Friede. In 1938, when Covici moved to the Viking Press, Steinbeck remained loyal and stayed with Covici. Covici reprinted Steinbeck's earlier books and edited the rest of his work.

But Steinbeck's California years became increasingly difficult as his books became more controversial. *In Dubious Battle* (1936), *Of Mice and Men* (1937), and particularly *The Grapes of Wrath* (1939) brought him great criticism and controversy.

Shortly after the publication of *The Grapes of Wrath*, he told *Los Angeles Times* reporter Tom Cameron, who his enemies were: "It isn't the refugees back there in Oklahoma," but rather "the big oil men and outfits like the Oklahoma Chamber of Commerce. If anyone's sore at me for the book it's that kind of people."

Steinbeck's phrase "that kind of people" would eventually include civic leaders from Steinbeck's home town of Salinas, the site of *The Long Valley* (1938), and would especially include the people of Monterey, whom Steinbeck introduced to the world with these lines in

Cannery Row: "Its inhabitants are, as the man once said, 'whores, pimps, gamblers, and sons of bitches,' by which he meant everybody." And until his death, it appears that many Californians never forgot that phrase, even though Steinbeck followed that with the line "saints and angels and martyrs and holy men," referring to the same people.

Cameron wrote: "Steinbeck's retreat to his hilltop citadel is not to protect himself from the wrath of the Okies, some of whom were working today in the orchards of the Los Gatos region, but is a flight from club program chairman and civic busybodies."

There are few existing interviews of Steinbeck during his California years. This is not surprising, considering the ordeal of publicity and vilification he endured during those years. He was shocked at the reception of his books, especially in California. In *John Steinbeck: The Voice of the Land*, Keith Ferrell summarized his anguish after the publication of *The Grapes of Wrath*: "The novel was popular, but it was also controversial. Book review sections might endorse the book's success, but many editorial pages attacked the novel and its author. Some editorialists damned Steinbeck's realism as radical and inflammatory. Negative reaction was particularly severe in California's agricultural areas and in many of Oklahoma's cities. People in both states felt that Steinbeck had maligned them. Some California farmers' groups worked to have the novel banned from schools and public libraries. Steinbeck's language, and his novel's blunt approach and presentation of sexuality, also sparked outrage."

What do we see in interviews with Steinbeck during this period? The few interviews that Steinbeck granted during these California years show him fearing for his safety (he had been warned not to travel alone; if he did, a sheriff might have him arrested on some trumped up charge). He and his first wife Carol had to fight desperately for their own privacy, in the face of a blizzard of requests to speak, or to donate profits from his books to needy individuals or organizations.

These early interviews also show Steinbeck feeling beleaguered by his own fame. He told writer Cameron: "There's getting to be a fictitious so-and-so out there in the public eye. He's a straw man and he bears my name. I don't like him—that straw man. He's not me—he's the Steinbeck the public has created out of its own imagination and thinks ought to be me."

More importantly, we see a writer who did not—then or later—embroider the fabric of his life. Steinbeck's interviews during his early, painful years in the cold glare of criticism and publicity remain remarkably honest. He was aware of the hazards of publicity and shied away from it, as his statement in the 1939 N.E.A. interview by John C. Rice shows: "I have always wondered why no author has survived a best-seller. Now I know. The publicity and fan-fare are just as bad as they would be for a boxer. One gets self-conscious and that's the end of one's writing."

In the mid-1940s, Steinbeck left California. Although he later visited the area to do research for *East of Eden* (published in 1952) and again much later during the research for *Travels with Charley* (1962), he never again lived for any length of time in California. In fact, *Cannery Row*, published in 1945, rekindled all the old hatreds (a word Steinbeck often used) in Monterey, where earlier *Tortilla Flat* had been branded by the local chamber of commerce as "a damned lie."

In the 1930s and early 1940s, we see him wrestling with success and controversy. The war was a watershed period. As the war began and progressed, the controversy about Steinbeck's earlier books faded from the public's attention. And, just as importantly, war plants on the west coast absorbed the migrant population into the workforce, thus resolving a crucial problem which had so occupied Steinbeck's attention, in his California novels.

His 1940 trip with his friend Ed Ricketts to the Mexican Gulf of California, which he preferred to call by its earlier name, the Sea of Cortez, was not only a research expedition which resulted in *The Sea of Cortez* and later *The Log from the Sea of Cortez* (1951), but was also an escape from the publicity and turmoil of his previous notoriety in California. The trip was literally and figuratively a flight from persecution.

During the war, Steinbeck worked as a correspondent for the New York *Herald Tribune* and his war reportage was later published as *Once There Was a War* (1958). He was also asked to write about the Air Force, and he researched and published *Bombs Away: The Story of a Bomber Team.* In typical Steinbeck fashion, he followed and wrote about the training of a bomber crew right up to their first bombing mission. Steinbeck refused to go on the mission and felt he could only write about what he had seen. He kept that straightforward honesty throughout his life, in private and in public.

After the war, he moved to New York City and later to Sag Harbor, Long Island. His baptism of acclaim largely over we see him more at ease with interviewers, often charming. It is interesting to see how often in these later interviews Steinbeck spoke of other matters in addition to writing, since by then he felt mostly freed of his controversial past.

The 1953 Associated Press interview with Charles Mercer is instructive for what we see of Steinbeck at 51. Such a relaxed interview would have been impossible earlier. We see Steinbeck dressed in the same kind of clothes he wore for the earlier 1930s interviews. His speech, we can judge, is slower, more introspective. He does not show the anger at the social system he revealed during his California years. A recurring subject during the later interviews is his discussion of his writing methods—and his perception of himself as seen by the critics.

Steinbeck deliberately did not follow book "A" with the same form and content. Book "B" might be more experimental in form or subject. Book "C" may not relate in any way to "A" or "B." For example, he published *Cannery Row*, a novel about the residents of the cannery area of Monterey, California, in 1945, followed that with *The Wayward Bus*, a novel about a journey toward self-enlightenment, in 1947, and *The Pearl*, a short novel about the consequences of greed, in 1947. His reportage *A Russian Journal* was published in 1948 and was seldom reprinted. And *Burning Bright*, a novel also written in the form of a stage-play, published in 1952 was his worst commercial and critical failure.

Also in 1952 he published his epic novel *East of Eden*, based on the Biblical story of Cain and Abel, and followed that with *Sweet Thursday* (1954), an unofficial sequel to *Cannery Row*. While many critics and reviewers could accept *Sweet Thursday* because of its relation to *Cannery Row*, few could accept *The Short Reign of Pippin IV*, Steinbeck's next book published in 1957, which was a satire on life in France during the years of Charles deGaulle. Many critics brutally ridiculed it, calling it thin and insignificant and suggesting it had no place in the Steinbeck canon.

These criticisms disturbed Steinbeck; he felt it was his right to always experiment with form and method and theme. He emphasized how unfair the criticism was that a book was a failure simply because it did not follow the form or theme of a previous book.

Steinbeck also regularly criticised the critics for being unable (or perhaps unwilling) to see "down through" his novels for layers of meaning, like the layers of an onion. Writing to Pat Covici in 1945, Steinbeck says: "It is interesting to me, Pat, that no critic has discovered the reasons for those little chapters in C.R. (*Cannery Row*) You would have known. Nearly all lay readers know. Only critics don't. Are they somehow the lowest common denominator? Far from being the sharpest readers, they are the dullest." Even in his Nobel Prize speech he touched on this: "Literature was not promulgated by a pale and emasculated critical priesthood singing their litanies in empty churches—nor is it a game for the cloistered elect, the tin-horn mendicants of low-calorie despair."

Throughout these interviews, especially in those he gave after World War Two, we continue to see Steinbeck as a private man. He did not lecture—he hated to give speeches. He refused to create a mythology for publicity or exhibit himself as an expert. Thus we see the man through these interviews, year after year, decade after decade, as honestly as he can express himself.

When Steinbeck won the Nobel Prize for Literature in 1962, his critics were given another chance to protest. Shortly after receiving the award, Arthur Mizener published a long essay in the *New York Times* titled "Does a Moral Vision of the Thirties Deserve A Nobel Prize?" (9 December 1962) His answer: No. Mizener's assessment hurt him deeply, and he never forgot and perhaps never forgave that kind of criticism. Years later he referred to critics as "the Mizeners of the world."

As he grew older, his perceptions changed. He published *The Winter of Our Discontent* in 1961, a novel about respectability in a small New England town; critics observed the tone and subject was far removed from the heated anger of his earlier *The Grapes of Wrath*, published in 1939. At a press conference in 1962, called the day after the announcement that he had won the Nobel Prize, he admitted he had changed. He said that he was probably no longer "annoyed at anything."

What *don't we see* in these later interviews? What subjects were not discussed—or perhaps not even recognized as important by the interviewers? We see little mention of Steinbeck's first two failed marriages, although there is mention of his successful marriage to his third wife, Elaine. We see little mention of his sons, Thom and John. Steinbeck biographies, such as Jackson Benson's *The True Adventures of John Steinbeck, Writer*, indicate that although Steinbeck loved his sons, he was apparently not the most diligent father in the world. Most importantly, the one key issue we don't see discussed in these interviews was Steinbeck's changing political viewpoint. From the days of *The Grapes of Wrath*, when he was considered a classic social liberal, he changed over the years until he eventually supported Lyndon Johnson and agreed with Johnson's Vietnam policies.

A series of articles he wrote from Vietnam for the newspaper *Newsday* divided his friends and readers. As Jackson Benson writes in *The True Adventures of John Steinbeck, Writer*, "Of course, many American reporters in Vietnam in 1966 tended to be hawkish, or at the very least sympathetic to the plight of the American soldier, but Steinbeck aroused the special ire of the antiwar Left as a 'traitor.' It was Steinbeck that they focused on and who became for them a symbol, a *cause celebre* to prosecute."

Some of his life-long friends never forgave him for that change, which they thought betrayed everything he had believed in during his earlier years. One of the issues which apparently separated Steinbeck from his sons was Vietnam. His son John published *In Touch* (Alfred Knopf, 1968), which was a younger man's negative view of Vietnam. Benson also writes: "He might have drawn special hatred also for his position in American culture. John Jr., in his book *In Touch*, speaks of his thinking of his father as 'a kind of American-conscience figure,' and it may be that he became so, and may even remain so, for many of the rest of us. If this is true, then it also explains the special antagonism that his judgment of the war as morally justified aroused in those who were convinced otherwise."

Steinbeck, Benson writes, returned the antagonism by referring to "the shiver of shame I sometimes feel at home when I see the Vietnicks, dirty clothes, dirty minds, sour smelling wastelings and their ill-favored and barren pad mates. Their shuffling drag-ass protests that they are conscience-bound not to kill people are a little silly. They're not in danger of that. Hell, they couldn't hit anybody."

This view, which caused Steinbeck's friends so much agony, is seldom brought up in interviews, and they just do not reflect the extent of his involvement with the Vietnam war. Perhaps reporters did not know of the anguish he caused his friends or did not think it diplomatic to broach the subject of Vietnam in an interview during those trying years. After he won the Nobel Prize, reporters may have felt even more reluctant to press him strongly about his views on the war. This subject was a key Steinbeck dilemma during his final years, just as it was the watershed issue during the administration of Lyndon Johnson.

Throughout his life, Steinbeck, as interview subject, remained remarkably straightforward; he shied away from details of his life, but did eventually answer most questions about himself. He did not wish to have his picture taken (and only much later did his picture appear on any of the dust jackets of his books). And he did not recreate his persona in fictional form. Nor did he weave half-truths about his life or create myths about himself. Ultimately, Steinbeck kept his own values, his own compass throughout his life: he insisted on his privacy; he did not become a public lecturer, and he chose to experiment in form and style from book to book.

As late as 1965, after he won the Nobel Prize for Literature, he told interviewer Herbert Kretzmer: "This business of being a celebrity has no reference to the thing I am interested in. And that is my work. I know of no sadder people than those who believe their own publicity. I still have my own vanities, but they have changed their face. Also, it's nobody's damn business how I live."

Here then, is John Steinbeck.

Interviews in this collection have not been edited since their original publication except to correct obvious typesetting errors. Headlines have been changed slightly to reflect the style in this series. Recurring questions have been retained to show similarities or differences in the answers over time.

An "interview" with Steinbeck in the *Paris Review*—Viking Press series *Writers at Work* has not been included in this collection. Although it appears to be a spontaneous interview, Steinbeck was too ill to participate in the project, and the quotations were collected from various sources, including *Steinbeck: A Life in Letters*.

The editor is grateful to the following individuals who helped with this book: Preston C. Beyer; Mary Jean S. Gamble, the John Steinbeck Library, Salinas, California; Tetsumaro Hayashi, the John Steinbeck Society, Ball State University, Muncie, Indiana, and Kiyoshi Nakayama, Kansai University, Japan.

Books cited in the introduction include: Jackson Benson, *The True Adventures of John Steinbeck, Writer* (New York: The Viking Press, 1984); Keith Ferrell, *John Steinbeck: The Voice of the Land* (New York: M. Evans and Co., 1986) and John Steinbeck IV, *In Touch* (New York: Alfred Knopf, 1968). Interview quotations cited in the introduction appear in full in the text.

This book is for Jean, with love.

Chronology

1902 John Ernst Steinbeck born, 27 February, in Salinas, California.

1919 Graduates from Salinas High School.

1920-25 Attends Stanford University; takes courses in English and Marine Science.

1924 Publishes in the Stanford University *Spectator*.

1925 Leaves Stanford without graduating. Travels to New York; works as a reporter for *The New York American* and works as a laborer building the original Madison Square Garden.

1926 Returns to California and begins writing.

1929 His first novel, *Cup of Gold* published by the firm of Robert M. McBride, New York.

1930 Marries Carol Henning and settles in Pacific Grove, California. Meets marine biologist Edward F. Ricketts, who becomes life-long friend. Begins selling his literary work through the McIntosh & Otis literary agency, New York. Will stay with McIntosh & Otis throughout his career.

1932 Second novel, *The Pastures of Heaven* published by Brewer, Warren & Putnam, New York. Lives in Los Angeles.

1933   Returns to Pacific Grove. His third novel, *To a God Unknown* published by Robert O. Ballou, New York.

1935   His fourth novel, *Tortilla Flat*, published by Covici-Friede, New York. He begins his association with editor/publisher Pascal Covici. Steinbeck will remain with Pascal Covici throughout his career. *Tortilla Flat* wins the Commonwealth Club of California Gold Medal.

1936   *In Dubious Battle* published by Covici-Friede. His series of newspaper articles about the plight of the migrant workers is published in *The San Francisco News* and reprinted as a pamphlet under the title *Their Blood Is Strong* in 1938. Many items and ideas from the series will later appear in *The Grapes of Wrath*. *In Dubious Battle* wins another Gold Medal from the Commonwealth Club of California.

1937   *Of Mice and Men* published as a novel in February; stage play begins New York run in November. The play wins the New York Drama Critics' Circle Award. Steinbeck travels to California with migrant workers. *Of Mice and Men* is distributed by the Book-of-the-Month Club, giving him his first financial success.

1938   Covici-Friede dissolved. Pascal Covici moves to the Viking Press as editor. Steinbeck will publish with Covici and the Viking Press for the rest of his life. *The Long Valley* is published.

1939   *The Grapes of Wrath* is published.

1940   *The Grapes of Wrath* wins the Pulitzer Prize. Steinbeck escapes the controversy surrounding *The Grapes of Wrath* by traveling to the Sea of Cortez with Ed Ricketts. He works on the film of *The Forgotten Village*.

1941 *Sea of Cortez: A Leisurely Journey of Travel and Research* is published: Steinbeck co-authored the book with Ed Ricketts. *The Forgotten Village* is published in book form. Film versions of *Of Mice and Men* and *The Grapes of Wrath* are distributed. Henry Fonda appears in lead role in film of *The Grapes of Wrath*.

1942 *Bombs Away: The Story of a Bomber Team* is published after Steinbeck is asked to write about the Army Air Corps. His anti-Nazi novel *The Moon Is Down* is published. He is divorced from Carol Henning.

1943 Marries Gwyndolen Conger. Becomes war correspondent for the New York *Herald Tribune*. *The Portable Steinbeck* is published with an Introduction by Pascal Covici.

1944 First son Thom is born. Steinbeck writes the script for the film *Lifeboat*.

1945 *Cannery Row* is published; main character is based on Ed Ricketts.

1946 Son John IV is born. *The Portable Steinbeck* is republished, with an Introduction by critic Lewis Gannett.

1947 *The Wayward Bus* and *The Pearl* are published. Steinbeck travels through Russia with war photographer Robert Capa.

1948 *A Russian Journal* is published, with photographs by Capa. Steinbeck is divorced from Gwyndolen Conger. Ed Ricketts dies when his car is struck by train. Steinbeck elected to the American Academy of Letters.

1949 Film version of *The Red Pony* is released.

1950   Film version of *Viva Zapata* is released, starring Marlon
        Brando. *Burning Bright* is published as a novel and stage
        play. It is his worst failure. Steinbeck marries Elaine Scott
        in December.

1951   Steinbeck republishes his *Sea of Cortez* under the title
        The Log from the Sea of Cortez with long essay about Ed
        Ricketts. Steinbecks live in New York City, with summer
        on Long Island.

1952   *East of Eden* is published.

1953   *The Short Novels of John Steinbeck* is published.

1954   *Sweet Thursday* is published, a sequel to *Cannery Row*.

1955   Rodgers and Hammerstein produce *Pipe Dream*, a
        musical based on *Sweet Thursday*.

1957   *The Short Reign of Pippin IV* is published, a satire on
        Gaullist France. Steinbeck travels to Mallory country in
        England.

1958   *Once There Was a War*, Steinbeck's collected war
        correspondence is published.

1959   Lives most of the year in England, studying the *Morte
        d'Arthur*.

1960   Travels through the U.S. in pickup truck, with French
        poodle Charley.

1961   *The Winter of Our Discontent* is published.

1962   Steinbeck receives the Nobel Prize for Literature. *Travels
        with Charley in Search of America* is published.

1963   Participates in Cultural Exchange visit behind the Iron Curtain with playwright Edward Albee.

1964   Receives the Presidential Medal of Freedom. Editor, publisher and friend Pascal Covici dies in October.

1966   *America and Americans* published, edited by Thomas Guinzburg.

1968   John Steinbeck dies in New York City, 20 December.

1969   *Journal of a Novel: The East of Eden Letters*, his diary of the progress of *East of Eden* is published.

1971   *The Portable Steinbeck* is republished, with an introduction by Pascal Covici, Jr.

1975   *Steinbeck: A Life in Letters* is published, edited by Elaine Steinbeck and Robert Walsten.

1976   *The Acts of King Arthur and His Noble Knights*, Steinbeck's version of the *Morte d'Arthur* is published by the firm Farrar, Straus and Giroux, New York.

Conversations with John Steinbeck

Sketching the Author
of *Tortilla Flat*
Ella Winter/1935

From *The San Francisco Chronicle*, 2 June 1935. Copyright ©
1935, *The San Francisco Chronicle*. Reprinted by permission.

John Steinbeck, whose charming story, "Tortilla Flat," was
published last week, does not like publicity. He likes it so little
that his publisher knows practically nothing about him. The
following story about him is the first appearance in print of any
details of his life.

Down out of the hills he came, he said; he felt as if he had somehow
always lived in them. And John Steinbeck looks as if he might have; of
giant height, sunburned, with fair hair and fair moustache and eyes
the blue of the Pacific on a sunny day, and a deep, quiet, slow voice.
He belongs to this Coast, the Monterey bay, the ranges and cliffs of
the Big Sur country. His father was born and lived most of his life in
Salinas where he remained a public official—County Treasurer—for
many years. He has just died. His mother taught in the tiny red school
house of the Big Sur 60 years ago.

He reminds one of Robinson Jeffers immediately; his height, his
blue eyes, his slow talk, his entwinement with the hills and stones,
canyons and people of this strange coast. He has never met Jeffers;
he hardly dares to because "his poetry is perfect to me, and I don't
think one should get the man mixed up with his work. I have tried to
get myself out of my own books, and I think I have just about
succeeded now."

His first books, *Pastures of Heaven* and *To a God Unknown*, are
about ranch people and the almost mystic love of land they nurse;
Tortilla Flat, just published, is a charmingly roguish story of the
paisanos—native Californians whose ancestry includes native and
American strains who live in the wooden-shacked "slums" above the
old sea town and drink and laze and philosophize and do good and

3

evil joyously as the days pass by. It is humorous, as his first books are not; but humour with a wise, light, almost wistful touch. One can't imagine Steinbeck either coarse or clumsy any more than one can imagine him hard, sophisticated or smart in the modern manner.

Steinbeck was born in Florida and lived there till his seventh or eighth year and then came West. [Steinbeck was born in California; the newspaper's statement is true of his father who had the same name.] Two of his sisters are much older than John; one was brought up with him. He went to Stanford off and on for eight years, but was only happy there when they accepted that he wasn't anxious for a degree and wanted to study only what interested him. Then they let him be.

He has been about a good bit; twice to New York, where he worked on a newspaper and got fired because he couldn't report facts, but only the poetry or philosophy he saw in the facts; where he helped carry bricks for the building of Madison Square Garden; where he worked as a chemist, painter's apprentice, laborer. He has lived at Lake Tahoe, where he took care of an estate in the silent, snowbound winter. His father, who wanted him to have all the chances he didn't have, gave his son a tiny pittance.

For some years now he has done nothing but write. John lives with his wife in a tiny dark brown frame house surrounded by many other brown and white and yellow frame houses, in a little dirt lane in Pacific Grove; the house is mostly hidden by honeysuckle and other creeping vines. Steinbeck's tall, black-haired and soft-voiced wife, Carol, who is from San Jose, comes out on the little porch to talk enthusiastically of John's work and their funny runaway marriage five years ago in Los Angeles and her historical research in the SERA in Monterey, and their boating on the bay. They have just bought Neil Weston's self-made launch—Edward Weston's son—for Neil is going to Japan on an old windjammer. Whenever they can, the Steinbecks go out in it and fish and sail. The fish are a valuable addition—or rather subtraction—from their budget, for they have been living for a long while on $25 a month.

Steinbeck reads a little fiction although he likes the writers who had leisure to think about what they really thought. He likes Thackeray, for instance, but he doesn't like Proust "because Proust was sick, he wrote his sickness and I don't like sick writing."

He doesn't seem to think you can explain much in words. "Everything is nonsense," he says. "We are on the verge of a new age, but how can anyone tell what it will be till it's here? And so everything anyone talks or writes or says is just nonsense." (This is very much Robinson Jeffers' attitude.) Steinbeck loves to read physics and philosophy and biology, however. "The biologists are on the verge of new discoveries that make a new world outlook." His blue eyes with their black pin-point pupils look far out, through you and the walls of the room and the eucalyptus and cypress hedge, way out over Point Lobos and those "possessed" hills and the ocean. Much of the time you feel he is divining something outside and beyond the mere earthly creatures sitting there and talking plain practical words.

He doesn't like publicity and he doesn't like photographs and he doesn't like personal fuss, not as a pose, but because they do you damage; get you in the way of your work; and because they seem so unimportant compared to the life in the hills out of which he came.

More a Mouse Than a Man, Steinbeck Faces Reporters
New York World Telegram/1937

From *New York World Telegram*, Friday, 23 April 1937

John Steinbeck, author of the best-selling *Of Mice and Men*, walked into the office of his publisher today with a tall bottle of brandy beneath his arm, planked it down on a wide table, and said:—

"All right, bring 'em on."

Mr. Steinbeck has suddenly become prominent enough in contemporary letters not to be afraid of interviewers. Certain it is he's big enough with his six-foot, brawny frame.

"But it's a fact," he said, "that I've been in an utter state of confusion since I got into town last week-end. Pat Covici wanted me to talk to reporters, but I said I wouldn't do it. Frankly, I was scared to death."

The brandy, however, brought back a portion of his courage, and he talked of his books, his coming journey to Europe, the coyotes that howl outside his California farmhouse, of the time he worked as a day laborer in the building of Madison Sq. Garden and of mice and men.

He recalled, too, how when he was in New York the time before—more than ten years ago—he got a job as a reporter in a desperate effort to make a living and was fired "because I couldn't write."

He went back to the little town of Los Gatos, in central California, where he has the farmhouse, and began writing novels. Now men like Heywood Broun and Alexander Woolcott are making large clanking sounds in the welkin about his work.

He and his wife, Carol, came from California by freighter. They selected one that would let them ashore in Philadelphia so they could ease the pain of coming into metropolitan New York.

"It's so damned big and noisy," said Mr. Steinbeck, "alongside the place we've got two miles out from Los Gatos, that it has had us both scared. I had to bring along this brandy, or I'd have died in a nervous collapse the minute you fellows started talking to me."

He has spent the week talking with stage designers and directors, because *Of Mice and Men* will be produced on Broadway by George S. Kaufman and Sam Harris next fall. Tonight he will go to the Peekskill farm of his publisher to write the play version of the book.

His latest novel doesn't please him.

"It's nothing but a trial horse—a copybook exercise," he explained. "I wrote it simply to develop a form. Yes, the form of a play. I had no idea how to write a play, but I experimented, and it looks as though it worked."

In his California farmhouse he keeps "office hours" to do his writing. Beyond that, he has few other interests. Does he fish and hunt?

"I've been trying to shoot a quail for five years," he said. "Every time I see one around the house I dash in and get the gun, and get it to my shoulder, and then I can't shoot. The minute I take a good look at a quail I can't kill it. They are such nice little birds."

He is deeply tanned, with the bluest eyes you've ever seen. He comes of German-Irish stock. As quickly as the play version of his book is finished, he and Carol will board another freighter for their trip abroad. They'll visit his relatives near Londonderry in Ireland.

"Then," he said, "We're going to get some bicycles and ride up through Sweden and then visit Russia. Why? No reason at all. Just to have fun. All the Russians I've known sang a damn good song when they had a few drinks, so I like Russians. I certainly have no thought of writing a book out of the trip."

Mr. Steinbeck says that all the characters in *Of Mice and Men*, *Tortilla Flat* and his other books have been people he has known. Occasionally one of his characters will be a composite of two personalities. As for the two principal characters in *Of Mice and Men* they were portrayed as they actually exist in California.

The shy Californian said that today was the first time he has ever been interviewed in his life.

"And be damned sure," he concluded, "that it's the last."

Men, Mice and Mr. Steinbeck

New York Times/1937

George S. Kaufman was in the library of his home one night last
Spring when his wife came down from the floor above with a thin
book in her hand. It was *Of Mice and Men*, and an hour later the
playwright was remarking:

"I don't know whether there's a dollar in it, but it's got to be
prepared for the stage and produced. Steinbeck's the man to do it. He
knows these people. I want to direct it. You thought of it first. Better
wire in the morning for the rights."

And so it came to pass that the following morning John Steinbeck,
on his small ranch in Los Gatos, Calif., got a telegram from his New
York agents announcing that Mr. Kaufman was enthusiastic and that
Mrs. Kaufman wanted an option on the dramatic rights. The book had
been out about ten days, had begun to receive extraordinarily
enthusiastic reviews and already there had been three or four wired
offers for the dramatic rights to it.

Mr. Steinbeck didn't hesitate a moment as to which to accept when
the magic name of "G.S.K." appeared in the offing. He wired an
acceptance and expressed the hope that the latter would make any
practical suggestions which might occur to him. Perhaps they could
meet, though he wouldn't be coming East until a few weeks later
when he and his wife were to take a freighter from New York for their
first European trip.

They didn't meet, actually, until after this jaunt was over in August.
Mr. Kaufman had a date to meet Moss Hart in California and found
that he would be traveling west by train while Mr. Steinbeck and his
wife would be coming east on a boat passing through the Panama
Canal.

They did exchange numerous letters. Mr. Kaufman outlined certain
ideas which he had in mind for the transfer of the story to the stage,

and Mr. Steinbeck began the actual writing within a week after the arrangement was consummated. Mr. Kaufman, in the meantime, had sent a copy of the book to Sam H. Harris in Florida and the latter had expressed his enthusiastic approval and his desire to participate in the production when it was ready.

The play took its final shape during a week which followed Mr. Steinbeck's European trip, a week which he spent at Mr. Kaufman's Pennsylvania estate. It was then that he told of what he had in mind when he wrote the book.

"My idea," he said to this correspondent, "was to write a play in the form of a novel. It was an experiment. I wanted to call it at first 'a play to be read.' I constructed it in scenes and filled in the character descriptions and painted in the background. Despite the fact that it has sold more than 150,000 copies, I don't consider that it was quite a success—as a play. The experiment flopped. By that I mean when I came up against a practical man of the theatre like Kaufman I found that I had to do a lot of extensive rewriting of the book itself."

As a matter of fact, Mr. Steinbeck rather exaggerated here. Practically 85 percent of the dialogue now spoken on the Music Box stage is to be found in the book. There have been some transpositions of scenes for dramatic effect and the introduction of one or two new incidents for the same reasons, but the basic essence of the book is in the acted play. Pressed for some comment upon the characters in the book, Mr. Steinbeck admitted that they were more or less drawn from actual life.

"I was a bindle-stiff myself for quite a spell," he said. "I worked in the same country that the story is laid in. The characters are composites to a certain extent. Lennie was a real person. He's in an insane asylum in California right now. I worked alongside him for many weeks. He didn't kill a girl. He killed a ranch foreman. Got sore because the boss had fired his pal and stuck a pitchfork right through his stomach. I hate to tell you how many times. I saw him do it. We couldn't stop him until it was too late."

Mr. Steinbeck didn't concern himself much with the casting of the play. Mr. Kaufman insisted that he see a few actors one afternoon, and he did so, but he found this end of the proceedings rather uninteresting.

"I don't go to the theatre much and I don't know a darn thing about actors," he commented. "Mr. Kaufman seems to know about all there is to know about that end of it. I'm quite content to leave it to him."

"And you won't be in New York for rehearsals, or for the opening performance?"

"Hell, no," he replied, "I've got work to do out in California. I can't work here in New York. I'll be setting out in the morning. Two days here are enough."

He stuck to his word. He's been on his California ranch ever since. A smudged letter received from him a few days ago contained this apology—"Just came off the prairie in a covered wagon, hence the finger smears." It is known, however, that since the play went into rehearsal three weeks and a half ago he has been evincing considerable interest. He even went so far as to instruct his publisher, Pascal Covici, to relay an act-by-act report on the opening over the long-distance telephone. He had to go to a friend's house to receive this as there isn't a phone on his own place. He also admitted that he might come on here for a look if the play developed into a good success.

Oklahomans Steinbeck's Theme
Louis Walther/1938

From *The San Jose Mercury News*, 8 January 1938. Reprinted with permission of *The San Jose Mercury News*.

John Steinbeck, virile author of *Tortilla Flat* and *Of Mice and Men*, now working at his home near Los Gatos on a novel which he calls "the Oklahomans," feels that today's migration of people from the dust bowl states to the west coast will profoundly alter the tenor of life in California.

"Their coming here now is going to change things almost as much as did the coming of the first American settlers," Steinbeck declared during an informal conversation in the kitchen of his white-walled foothill home.

First gaining fame with the publication of *Tortilla Flat*, a story of an out-of-the-way Mexican settlement in Monterey, a few years ago, John Steinbeck today is one of the best known of the younger writers, and was recently included in "America's Young Men," a "Who's Who" of the younger men of the country.

Except for a friend who had walked in to visit him the day before, he was alone at the place. His wife, the former Carol Henning of San Jose, is in New York taking care of arrangements for the opening of *Tortilla Flat* Thursday at the Hudson theater, he explained.

The play, being produced by Grisel and Kirkland, was adapted to the stage by Jack Kirkland from Steinbeck's first famous novel. Kirkland dramatized *Tobacco Road*.

"I think it'll flop," Steinbeck predicted calmly.

"Kirkland's got a pretty good opening, though," he admitted. "He's reversed the theme of *Tobacco Road*. There he had a family which disintegrated because they lost their land. In *Tortilla Flat*, he pictures a family which disintegrates when they get some property."

Steinbeck is a big man with thick shoulders, frank blue eyes, and dark hair that curls up from his forehead. He was dressed in gray sweatshirt, sailor-like wide bottomed blue jeans, and scarred leather moccasins.

He took a pot off the glistening white kitchen range and poured three cups of coffee. Letting a stream of evaporated milk run into his own cup, he continued his observations in regard to California's most recent immigrants, the people with whom he deals in "The Oklahomans," and with whom he has spent weeks working as a laborer on ranches up and down the state.

"These people have that same vitality that the original Americans who came here had," he said; "and they know just what they want.

"The Californian doesn't know what he does want. He wants things. The Oklahoman knows just exactly what he wants. He wants a piece of land. And he goes after it and gets it.

"California will be a better state for his coming," he added.

"Politics here will be more liberal, for one thing," he explained in answer to a question.

Steinbeck poured a brown paper full of tobacco, and rolled a cigarette.

"They can think straight beautifully," he went on. "I love that thing which happened down at Bakersfield. Some of the older ones wanted to hear a Holy Roller preacher. The younger ones didn't; so they had a meeting to decide the thing.

"They came to the conclusion that anyone who wanted to could preach in the camp; but that no one could take up a collection. It didn't take them long to get to the bottom of the thing," he chuckled.

The Oklahomans, too—and as he uses the word he means any of the southern dust bowl immigrants—are, according to Steinbeck, better farmers. They'll work harder and are less likely to fail.

The naive directness, the rich imagery and warm colorful dialect which are about the things Oklahomans bring with them, they will retain, though in modified form, he believes.

Socially, too, they will affect the country, he contends, pointing out, for instance, that they are likely to have larger families.

"The Oklahomans," which is going to be a rather long novel, is still a long way from finished, the author said. What his next work will be he does not know; but thinks he will return to the objective form employed in *Of Mice and Men*.

"I still think it's a good form even if I did make a failure of it here," he said.

Asked what he meant by the word failure in connection with a novel in its sixth edition, one whose stage version is now enjoying phenomenal success at the Music Box theater in New York, where it opened November 23, he explained:

"I wanted it to play from the lines. I was trying to write a book which could be acted directly. But I failed to do it. I had to re-write it for the stage."

His frank admission of what he considered a failure is apparently typical of Steinbeck. He seems most unassuming. Though affable and kindly, he dislikes interviews, shies away from personal questions and absolutely refuses to be photographed.

His home, Arroya del Ajo, is difficult to find even for one who has been shown the way. It is a low white house, nearly hidden by oaks, on a slope overlooking the Santa Clara valley. A high redwood stake fence makes the place yet more secluded.

Still only 37 years of age, Steinbeck has published three widely known novels, *Tortilla Flat*, *In Dubious Battle*, and *Of Mice and Men*. First editions of *Tortilla Flat* are said to be bringing $7 a volume.

An earlier work, *The Red Pony*, depicting three episodes of a boy's life, was recently brought out by Covici-Friede in hand-set type on hand-made paper at $10 a volume.

"A girl who grew up on the same block as I did in Salinas once accused me of giving a distorted picture of life by writing too much about mental 'defectives,'" he said. "I asked her if she remembered the little boy who had lived next door to us."

One by one he pointed out to her that 17 mental defectives lived on that one block in Salinas.

In "The Oklahomans," however, he said, there are no mental defectives. Among a people who undergo the hardships that they do the unfit do not survive.

Steinbeck thinks that both the novel and the play have something to offer each other. He thinks that the play can benefit by the descriptive color of the novel, and that the novel can benefit by the discipline of the play. That is what he expects to work toward when he finishes his present book.

"In the story I told how the pony got thinner and thinner. In the book the illustrator drew as fat and chunky a pony as you could imagine," he smiled.

Asked whether Lennie, the big blundering half-wit in *Of Mice and Men* was not symbolic in character, Steinbeck replied that all fiction characters are symbolic in that they represent human needs and human desires, but that Lennie was no more symbolic than other characters of the book.

John Steinbeck Turns His Wrath on *The Grapes of Wrath* Publicity

John C. Rice/1939

Newspaper Enterprise Association (June 1939). Reprinted by permission of Newspaper Enterprise Association.

SAN FRANCISCO—Big, solid, blue-eyed John Ernest Steinbeck today is one of America's foremost authors by grace of a 15-year-old decision to give up a promising boxing career in favor of writing.

It was a hard choice to make. Steinbeck was just out of college.

"I would have been a good boxer," he says. "I have the build and the speed, but my uncle talked me out of it. He kept reminding me how it would feel to be pinched and pulled at by sportswriters and trainers, to be on the platform before a bunch of yelling fans, and to have to sacrifice my personal privacy."

That cinched it. Steinbeck has always been jealous of his own freedom and privacy and he gave up any idea of chasing a professional crown. Now, however, he is not so sure he can keep away from the publicity—which he says he detests.

His most recent novel, *The Grapes of Wrath* is in its fifth printing a little more than a month after publication. This popularity has already had its effects on Steinbeck's life, and he isn't liking it at all.

"I have always wondered why no author has survived a best-seller," he grumbles. "Now I know. The publicity and fan-fare are just as bad as they would be for a boxer. One gets self-conscious and that's the end of one's writing."

The former California farmboy has always disliked limelight. He avoids speeches and banquets. He lives on a secluded ranch in the mountains south of San Francisco with his wife and dog, Bruga.

"But they get to me anyway. I get 30 or 40 letters a day from all sorts of people. They all want to make some sort of a freak out of me. They want to give me an individual importance which would destroy everything that I want to do with my work."

Steinbeck is neither aloof nor mysterious. He is friendly, hospitable and always glad of a chance to make a new friend. He loves to talk with people—all sorts of people.

That's the key to his character. He is interested in everything. Nothing bores him, nothing pleases him so much as a good laugh.

Since childhood he has tried his hand at everything from newspaperwork to acting as nursemaid in a fish hatchery. He has been a chemist in a sugar analysis laboratory, a watchman, a straw boss. He has carried bricks, run a cultivator, bucked grain bags—and he always comes back for more.

The Steinbeck ranch, atop a beautifully forested hill, commands a sweeping view of Santa Clara County farm lands and wooded knolls.

The house itself was designed and decorated by Mrs. Steinbeck, the former Carol Henning of San Jose, Calif. It is of Spanish-type architecture with large windows and big airy rooms. The furniture is comfortable and colorful. The walls are hung with bright Mexican tapestries and handsome prints.

Center of the Steinbecks' life is their combination swimming pool and reservoir. When friends come for a swim, the hospitable author provides ample supplies of beer which he deposits on the bottom of the pool to "keep it cool."

Steinbeck is 37, but admits that mechanical toys are his favorite amusement. That's why he likes the San Francisco Exposition—"It's all one big toy." Another favorite hobby is fishing, ocean fishing.

Steinbeck at work is another picture. It took him six months to write the 200,000 word *Grapes of Wrath*. "I put in a good working day," he says, "and usually get out about 2000 words." His chief cause of envy is his close friend, William Saroyan, who, he claims, never gets up from work from the time he starts a story until it is finished.

One of Steinbeck's big difficulties has always been spelling and punctuation.

"I used to have a terrible time," he says, "but since I have been married my wife copyreads all my work. She's wonderful—never misses a thing."

Steinbeck's major interest, it really amounts to a passion, is the problem of the migratory laborers in California. He writes about them, works for them, and gives them a major part of his income.

"They are getting some relief, now," he says almost fiercely, "but there must be more. Nothing permanent can be done for them now because we are in a period of transition much like the British industrial revolution.

"Imagine a situation in which employers think 20 cents an hour is over-pay and try to get the standard lower. One thing that would help a lot would be an information service with a weekly bulletin telling how many men are needed and where."

The Grapes of Wrath Author Guards Self from Threats at Moody Gulch

Tom Cameron/1939

LOS GATOS, July 8. —John Steinbeck, author of the best-selling novel, *The Grapes of Wrath*, has betaken himself to Moody Gulch, a secluded canyon three miles from here, and padlocked himself against the world.

For the first time in his career, Steinbeck is inaccessible to friend and enemy alike.

They will tell you in Los Gatos that Steinbeck has both—especially since his controversial odyssey of the Okies (Oklahoma dustbowl emigres now scattered about California) reached the bookstands.

There are two versions why.

Some Los Gatos folk and others say that Steinbeck, who took the title of his chronicle of the dust bowl emigres from Julia Ward Howe's "Battle Hymn of the Republic," has himself trampled out a bitter vintage of wrath—the enmity of the bewildered refugees from poverty and hunger whose cause he pleaded.

There have been reports of threats against the author which induced him to retreat to an almost inaccessible citadel—a refugee from the very economic refugees he sought to befriend.

Steinbeck gave me his own version. Here it is:

"Everything the people admire it destroys. It imposes a personality upon him it thinks he should have—whether that personality fits him or no, it doesn't seem to matter.

"There's getting to be a fictitious so-and-so (Steinbeck speaks as frankly as he writes) out there in the public eye. He's a straw man, and he bears my name.

"I don't like him—that straw man," Steinbeck complained. "He's not me—he's the Steinbeck the public has created out of its own imagination and thinks ought to be me."

Steinbeck has a double-barreled plan for protecting himself. It is, first, to keep strictly away from the public, and second, to "let the straw man stand out in front and take it."

Steinbeck disclaimed receiving many threatening letters from the Okies (the refugees are so called because many of them came from the Oklahoma dustbowl country,) as had been reported.

"It isn't the refugees who have taken exception to what I wrote," he asserted. "It's the moneyed people back there in Oklahoma—the big oil men and outfits like the Oklahoma City Chamber of Commerce. If anybody's sore at me for the book it's that kind of people."

Steinbeck's blue eyes flashed as he recalled some of the things said and printed about him.

"Somebody spread it all over that I was drunk in New York three weeks ago and was going around with my suspenders hanging down. Well I don't wear suspenders, and what's more I wasn't in New York at that particular time."

Steinbeck's temper rose again at mention of a recent attack in the columns of a newspaper chain. As he gathered himself to frame a sufficiently blistering retort, his wife reminded him of his condition (he had just had his tonsils removed to correct a sciatic condition from which he limps) and ordered him to keep his voice down to a whisper.

Regarding the report that Ruth Comfort Mitchell planned to write a refutation of some of the statements in his book, Steinbeck laughed in scorn.

"I know what I was talking about. I lived, off and on, with those Okies for the last three years. Anyone who tried to refute me will just become ridiculous."

Steinbeck's retreat to his hilltop citadel is not to protect himself from the wrath of the Okies, some of whom were working today in the orchards of the Los Gatos region, but is a flight from club program chairmen and civic busybodies, he insisted.

"Why do they think a writer, just because he can write, will make a good after-dinner speaker, or a club committee man—or even a public leader?" he asked.

"Just because Henry Ford made a good car, they wanted to run him for President. That's silly—unless he happened to be equipped for the other job as well.

"I'm no public speaker, and don't want to be. I'm not even a finished writer, yet. I haven't learned my craft.

"A writer, anyway, is just one step above a buffoon—an entertainer. If the public makes him think he is really somebody it destroys him. He pontificates, and that's the end of him.

"They're not going to lionize me. I think of the Arabian story-tellers, the best writers in the world. You didn't find them installed in luxurious surroundings. They squatted in the market places and told and retold their stories until they refined and perfected them to the point you find in the "Arabian Nights Entertainments."

"That's one reason you're not going to get a photograph of me—nobody is going to exploit me," Steinbeck said. "I don't want my face to be known. As soon as I get over this condition (he indicated his sore throat and his limp) I'll be out on the road again, sleeping in a ditch or somewhere, getting material for another yarn.

"Show you the letters from my friends, the Okies?" he echoed. "No, I don't do that. But I've got them—lots of them!

"Here—I'll show you what some of the Okies think of me. Carol, get that gingham dog they sent. They made that out of their shirt-tails or whatever scraps of cloth they could spare. That ought to convince you the Okies aren't after me."

The stuffed dog, made of vari-colored little squares of cloth, bore around its neck a tag reading, "Migrant John."

"And no pictures of this house, either," Steinbeck asserted as his visitors prepared to depart. And standing there in faded dungarees and touseled hair, square-shouldered Steinbeck, despite his limp, was prepared to enforce his edict, if necessary.

It wasn't.

After all, a man's home is his castle. Steinbeck, shunning his fellows for one of two reasons—and we've given you both versions—is no publicity-seeking Hollywood idol.

Voltaire Didn't Like Anything: A 1939 Interview with John Steinbeck

Robert DeMott/1986

From *The Steinbeck Quarterly* (Winter-Spring 1986), pp. 5-11. Reprinted with permission of *The Steinbeck Quarterly*.

Although John Steinbeck increasingly became a figure of public interest after the appearance of *Of Mice and Men* in 1937, the published record of his responses to direct questions from interviewers is generally confined to short interviews and group press meetings that he granted to members of the media, including journalists, newspaper reporters, and columnists. In fact, interviews with Steinbeck—one of the more popular novelists of his age—are still essentially fugitive items, widely scattered and often difficult to obtain. Furthermore, final literary interviews, conducted one-on-one by a knowledgeable interrogator, are almost nonexistent. Even Steinbeck's inclusion in *The Paris Review*'s famous "Art of Fiction" interview series is not, properly speaking, an interview at all, but a patchwork job made up of excerpts from the posthumous *Journal of a Novel* (1969) and *Steinbeck: A Life in Letters* (1975).

The section reproduced below from a 1939 thesis on Steinbeck—the first graduate thesis ever written about him—is actually a questionnaire; however, because Steinbeck responded individually to various queries about his life and art, it may be considered an interview, rather than a biographical sketch, a reminiscence, or an "impression," as Martin Bidwell termed his 1938 *Prairie Schooner* piece on Steinbeck. As such, Merle Danford's investigation stands as one of the first systematic attempts to induce the reclusive Steinbeck to cross the line between private artist and public persona. Despite Steinbeck's reluctance to elaborate the details of his biography, and his general hostility and suspiciousness toward the critical act itself, Danford's document ought to prove, at the very least, entertaining to readers of the *Steinbeck Quarterly*. In July 1938, when Steinbeck was living on Greenwood Lane in Los Gatos, California, and pushing hard against a variety of psychological, domestic, and financial pressures to maintain his daily output of two thousand words of *The Grapes of Wrath*, he received a letter from C.N. Mackinnon, a professor of English at Ohio University (Athens, Ohio). Mackinnon informed Steinbeck that Merle Danford, a graduate student at Ohio, was planning to write a master's thesis on Steinbeck; apparently, Mackinnon also requested permission for Danford to contact Steinbeck directly for additional information and biographical details.

In his reply, Steinbeck registered "dismay" of the "academic decay such a thesis indicates," but grudgingly conceded that he was "flattered" and "pleased to have her evaluate [his] work." He didn't know himself what it was about, Steinbeck admitted, "but maybe she will." In regard to answering her questions, Steinbeck warned:

> Let your young woman write, but let her beware, I'll lie—not because I want to lie, but because I can't remember what is true and what isn't. I'm reasonably sure that my biography, particularly when it is autobiography, is the worst pack of lies in the world. And the awful thing is that I don't know which are lies and which aren't. Compensation maybe, I don't know. It's so bad that my wife, who is a truthful person, really likes the truth I mean and puts some store in it, is all confused too. For years she struggled to keep her head above water, but she is sinking finally. I'm really sorry about this, but your candidate will just have to take her chance. I'm not trying to be funny—this is a tragic truth.

Armed with this *caveat*, Danford wrote a preliminary letter to Steinbeck. In his diary for Wednesday, 17 August 1938, Steinbeck noted, "The lady who is doing the thesis writes fearfully." Later that year, sometime in the fall, Danford finally sent her questionnaire to Steinbeck. Reviews of *The Long Valley* had begun to appear in major publications in the latter half of September 1938, and Danford excerpted several of them for Steinbeck's reactions. By the time Steinbeck addressed himself to her questions, he had completed *The Grapes of Wrath*, which he described to Danford as an "attempt to write the movement of the dust bowlers to California." Although he was emotionally spent from his long haul on the novel, and exceedingly short-tempered with people who continued to make unreasonable and unsolicited demands on his time and energy, Steinbeck did fulfill the letter of his promise to Danford.

His answers are published here for the first time, desultory as they are, they reveal that mixture of candor, self-effacement, flippancy, and irony characteristic of Steinbeck's defensive attitude toward his life and work. If Steinbeck is recalcitrant about providing biographical information (there are no surprises here in that arena, but then there are no "lies" either), he does offer a few useful revelations about writers he admired, and a humorous, if truculent, running commentary on several critics and reviewers. Finally, though Danford's questionnaire is not a pristine example of the interviewer's art, it is still a useful document, and one which adds some additional corroboration to this aspect of the novelist's elusive personality, already admirably recreated by Steinbeck's best biographer: "Biographical reference books, reporters, and graduate students could get nothing or nothing of consequence from him."

QUESTIONNAIRE

Place and date of birth?
    a. Salinas, California, 1902.
Nationality?
    a. Irish and German.
Who is your best biographer?
    a. Haven't any as far as I know.
During what years were you in New York City?
    a. 1925 I think.
For what papers were you reporter?
    a. They would deny it. Don't want to tell.
Which is your favorite literary creation?
    a. *War and Peace.*
Did you have a common model for such characters as Lennie, Johnny Bear, and Tulerecito?
    a. No—they are all stories I either knew or heard. Sort of folk tales. You'll find their counterparts in all folklore.
What actor turned down the part of Danny in Tortilla Flat *as too undignified for him?*
    a. I don't know. It was only hearsay.
Have any of your writings been filmed?
    a. No.

What qualities in Robinson Jeffers appeal most to you?

a. Can't answer this one. I'm no critic. I like the "Roan Stallion," "The Loving Shepherdess," and "The Tower Beyond Tragedy."

What are you willing to tell about the "big book," mentioned in Professor Mackinnon's letter?

a. All done now. An attempt to write the movement of the dust bowlers to California.

Have you any recognition in England?

a. My books are printed there, but I've never heard of them again. One Scottish reviewer says I write "pretty good English for an American."

Since you chose the phrase "In dubious battle" from Paradise Lost *and used the Round Table idea in* Tortilla Flat, *may we infer that you read much Milton and Tennyson?*

a. Have—of course. Round Table, not so much Tennyson as Geoffrey of Monmouth and Malory.

True or False

You attended Leland Stanford at intervals during an eight-year period but were not interested in and did not receive a degree.

a. More or less true.

You read little fiction, but you like Thackeray's work.

a. Sure I like Thackeray, but I like a hundred others.

You were fired from newspaper jobs because you dodged facts and put in philosophy and poetry to fit the situations.

a. False. Fired because I was a lousy reporter.

Ben Abramson, Chicago bookdealer, was the first Steinbeck "enthusiast."

a. First bookseller anyway—but don't forget I had had publishers who were at least temporarily enthusiastic. They were cured by the sale.

You're not really so fond of the wine jug; you use it as a device whereby you collect material from others.

a. I don't drink often; but when I do, I try to drink to excess if I can.

You were well pleased with Broderick Crawford's portrayal of Lennie, with John F. Hamilton as Candy, with Wallace Ford as George, with Claire Luce as the harlot.

a. Never saw them.

I should designate as a "common denominator" for your diversified writings the depicting of the submerged character.

a. Never thought of them as submerged.

Please comment on the following:

My deduction of your theory is (a) swinging away from the hectic, modern pace, and a turning to a less complex existence; (b) an acceptance of the beauty and ugliness of life; (c) "one must work toward something"—as Jim Nolan phrased it in In Dubious Battle.

a. Look! This is too complicated. I just write stories. Two stories may each have its own theory.

John Chamberlain ranks Tortilla Flat *and* In Dubious Battle *better writings than* Of Mice and Men.

a. I must pass up the next series. I don't often read criticism of my work and when I do I find it confusing. When criticism is evaluation I can't follow it and where it is interpretation, it is still screwy. I have often seen two critics interpret in opposite directions. Finally, I think criticism has no emphasis for the writer. If it is disciplinary as Krutch's seems to be, it disciplines a work already done and what can the writer do with interpretation of his own work.

Joseph Wood Krutch's criticism that Of Mice and Men *was as shamelessly "cooked up" as the death of Little Nell—a pure literary device.*

a. I wonder where he can find a literary work that is not "cooked up." This "cooked up" business is the latest critical phrase. There is a new one every year.

Krutch's statement that the public wants, not aristocracy, profanity, and sex, but the toughness, violence, and soupcon of social criticism Steinbeck supplies.

a. Krutch's knowledge of what the public wants is profound.

Ralph Thompson in The New York Times *calls "The Chrysanthemums" a "fumbling" story.*

a. Another critic's word. The woman was fumbling, but I knew what I was doing.

Stanley Young in The New York Times—*"Voltaire would have loved Katy the pig, but Disney will get her."*

a. Again a critic projects himself. Voltaire didn't like anything.
Elmer Davis in The Saturday Review of Literature—*reviewing* The
Long Valley—*writes: "In this collection there is less variety than you
would expect after Steinbeck's last three novels. The one off the trail
story is a burlesque hagiography, which might better have been left in
private circulation."*

a. I bet he's proud of that "hagiography" and the S.R.L. too. The
last retreat of the polysyllablists.

Ralph Thompson in The New York Times *writes: "The 'Johnny Bear'
story is dramatic, but hardly scrupulous. I pray that Mr. Steinbeck will
avoid fools, imbeciles, and boneheads in the future. He does better
with people who are normal or who can pass for such in a sizable
crowd. The best stories of* The Long Valley *are those dealing with
Jody."*

a. Mr. Thompson sets rather a task in his second sentence. How
can I? There aren't any more in my books than in the scene around
me.

Clifton Fadiman in The New Yorker *states: "The four stories ("The
Chrysanthemums," "The White Quail," "Breakfast," "The Harness")
are beautifully written, though I think Mr. Steinbeck is trying a mite
too hard to be sensitive and open to beauty."*

a. Might it not be that Mr. Fadiman is trying a mite too hard to
be—well an N.B.C. realist.

Edmund C. Richards in a North American Review *article stated that
the author's own philosophy of life seems always to be stated by Pilon
in* Tortilla Flat.

a. What the hell is this? What is your philosophy for instance? What
is Mr. Richard's philosophy? This is meaningless.

*Richards also speaks of your revolting against Puritanism, and of your
having a religion built on mysticism.*

a. I haven't heard this one for ten years. Used to be said about
everyone.

*Lewis Gannett in writing of his brief visit with you told of your meeting
a fabulous uncle and a still more fabulous aunt.*

a. Comes from India, riding on an elephant—mystic—wonderful.
The elephant wears the samite.

An article in Wilson Bulletin for Librarians *(March 1937) mentioned*

your being comparable with D.H. Lawrence because each of you
recognizes the inscrutable law of the instincts.

a. Also comparable because I have two legs, and a research will
show this to be the identical number Lawrence had.

"For two years Mr. Steinbeck was caretaker of a Lake Tahoe estate.
He was snowed in for eight months of the year. Here his hates were
melted away and he became able to write The Pastures of Heaven, *a*
story of people in the Gabilan Mountains."

a. O.K. as far as the first. After that it is a publisher's blurb. I still hate
plenty of people.

Dear Miss Danford:

I haven't wanted to be flippant. The curious hocus-pocus of
criticism I can't take seriously. It consists in squirreling up some odd
phrases and then waiting for a book to come running by.

And as to the questions as to what I mean by—or what my
philosophy is—I haven't the least idea. And if I told you one, it
wouldn't be true. I don't like people to be hurt or hungry or
unnecessarily sad. It's just about as simple as that. Sorry I can't go into
an erodite discussion. I could if I hadn't promised to be straight with
you. I hope this wasn't just a mess to you.

Sincerely,
John Steinbeck

John Steinbeck: Novelist at Work

Lewis Gannett/1945

Critics have had a holiday detecting exotic symbolisms in John Steinbeck's work. Perhaps they are there. He would be the last man to affirm or to deny it. To inquirers for biographical data he has been known to reply: "Please feel free to make up your own facts about me as you need them. I can't remember how much of me really happened and how much I invented. . . Biography by its very nature must be half fiction."

Nonetheless, in John Steinbeck's letters to his literary agents, McIntosh and Otis, covering almost fifteen years of partnership in creative writing, appears a singularly honest and revealing record of what John Steinbeck himself thought about what he was writing, when he was writing it.

Steinbeck has been interested in writing as long as he can remember. When he was four, he discovered, to his flabbergasted delight, that "high" rhymed with "fly," and from that day to this the permutations and combinations of words have charmed and fascinated him. He wrote for the Salinas, California, high school paper, *El Gabilan*, in 1919, when he was president of the senior class and on the basketball and track teams. He wrote during his intermittent sessions at Stanford University. In the early 1920's he functioned briefly as a reporter for the *New York Journal*, but he didn't like that; he wanted to do his own kind of writing. He wrote hard for almost fifteen years before he had his first success. He has always written more than he has published. Indeed, he destroyed two full-length novels before *Cup of Gold*, his first published novel, made its appearance in 1929.

It was in 1930 that Steinbeck began his long association with his literary agency. It was a new firm then, consisting of Mavis McIntosh and Elizabeth Otis, with Annie Laurie Williams as associated theatrical agent. Mary Squire Abbott joined the firm in 1931, Mildred Lyman several years later, and in the 1940's Miss McIntosh left. The firm's office became John Steinbeck's office and home whenever he was in New York. In his early years he consulted its partners for literary advice and sometimes for literary consolation. In later years the firm became his bookkeepers, his guards against an intrusive public, and most important of all, his friends.

His letters, at first shyly impersonal, grow increasingly warm; eventually they become comfortable, casual, intimate, family letters. The agents believed in Steinbeck from the first, they tried, mostly in vain, to market his early stories. But Steinbeck no more lost faith in them than they in him; in fact, at times he seems to have had more faith in his agents than in himself.

"I think I told you that the imperfections of *The Unknown God* [an earlier version of *To a God Unknown*] had bothered me ever since I first submitted the book for publication," the young author wrote in August, 1931, before his agents had succeeded in marketing any book of his. "Your announcement of the book's failure to find a public is neither unwelcome nor unpleasant to me. . . . I shall rewrite it. Whether my idea of excellence coincides with editors' ideas remains to be seen. Certainly I shall make no effort to 'popularize' the story . . . Thank you for your help. I am an unprofitable client."

Times changes. Six years later, when the tide had turned, Steinbeck wrote a brief note to the same agents: "Dear All: Acknowledging another check. Since I took your course I have sold. Do you want a testimonial?" Many authors, when success comes to them, shift restlessly from one agent and from one publisher to another. Steinbeck has never left a publisher who remained interested in his work; he has never had any agent but McIntosh and Otis.

Pastures of Heaven, Steinbeck's second published book, had a rather bewildering publishing history due to an epidemic of upsets in the New York book world. Robert Ballou, editor for Cape and Smith when he first saw the manuscript, recognized the quality of the book on first reading and accepted it with enthusiasm. Even before it had appeared in America, he wrote Martin Secker of London that it was "one of the most distinguished novels I have ever read in manuscript."

Before *Pastures of Heaven* appeared, Steinbeck had written several drafts of *To a God Unknown*, which no publisher then wanted. He had also finished a book called *Dissonant Symphony*, which was equally unmarketable; this he later withdrew, saying that, on rereading, he was ashamed of it. He had even written a murder mystery which he thought "might help pay for coffee." He had been groping, experimenting, finding his way. In *Pastures* he first struck what was to become known as the Steinbeck vein.

He announced his theme early in 1931. "There is, about twelve miles from Monterey, a valley in the hills called Corral de Tierra," he wrote. "Because I am using some of its people I am calling it Las Pasturas del Cielo. The valley was for years known as the happy valley because of the unique harmony which existed among its twenty families. They are ordinary people, ill educated but honest, and as kindly as any. In fact, in their whole history I cannot find that they have committed a really malicious act or an act which was not dictated by humble expediency or out-and-out altruism. There have been two murders, a suicide, many quarrels and a great deal of unhappiness in the pastures of Heaven, and all of these things can be traced to the influence of the A------s. So much is true. I am using the following method. The manuscript is made up of stories, each one complete in itself, having its rise, climax and ending. Each story deals with a family or an individual. They are tied together only by the common locality and the common contact with the A------s. I am trying to show this peculiar evil cloud which follows the A------s. Some of the stories are very short and some as long as 15,000 words . . . I wonder whether you think this a good plan."

McIntosh and Otis didn't keep carbons in those days, and there is no record to show whether they thought it a good plan. The book, of course, turned out a little differently; everything Steinbeck has ever written has grown and changed in the process of coming to birth. He learns a good deal about his stories, and his characters, in the process of writing.

Pastures of Heaven appeared in 1932; it had a friendly critical reception, but sold few copies. *To a God Unknown* appeared in 1933; it sold even less well. Robert Ballou had to "remainder" the unsold copies of both books, and neither sold even as well as *Cup of Gold*. When, after the success of *Tortilla Flat* in 1935, Pascal Covici bought the remaining unbound sheets and took over rights to the two books, he discovered to his amazement that the sales had not paid even for the pitifully small advances made to Steinbeck. With three published books, Steinbeck's total sales were fewer than three thousand.

Steinbeck never expected large sales; all his later successes surprised him. When he sent the final version of *To a God Unknown* to his agents, in February, 1933, he explained: "The book was hellish hard to write. I had been making notes on it for about five years. It will probably be a hard book to sell. Its characters are not 'home folks.' They make no more attempt at being human than the people in the Illiad. Boileau insisted that only gods, kings and heroes are worth writing about. I firmly believe that. The detailed accounts of the lives of clerks don't interest me much unless, of course, the clerk breaks into heroism. But I have no intention of trying to explain my book. It has to do that for itself. I would be sure of its effect if it could be stipulated that the reader read to an obbligato of Bach."

At that time Steinbeck was so poor that he could not even afford a dog. He had had a big dog named Omar as a companion when, a hermit in the high Sierras, he wrote *Cup of Gold*. The first letter from him in the McIntosh and Otis files, after explaining the project for *Pastures of Heaven*, continued to report that "Tillie Eulenspiegel the Airedale has puppies, as sinful a crew as ever ruined rugs. Four of them found your letter and ate all of it but the address. I should imagine they were awed by the address if I had not learned that they hold nothing in reverence. At present they are out eating each other."

But in 1933 he needed a dog. That was the year he reread his manuscript of *Dissonant Symphony* and hastened to advise New York that he wanted it killed. "I reread my copy and was ashamed of it," he wrote. "The Murder I thought might be sold to a pulp if it were cut down. Even a little money would be better than a bundle of paper. We are very happy. I need a dog pretty badly. I dreamed of great numbers of dogs last night. They sat in a circle and looked at me and I wanted all of them. Apparently we are headed for the rocks. The light company is going to turn off the power in a few days but we don't care

much. The rent is up pretty soon and then we shall move, I don't
know where."

He was writing *Tortilla Flat* then, and, strange as that seems today,
Tortilla Flat also proved hard to market. There is a tradition in
Steinbeck's agents' office that eleven publishers rejected it, but the
files preserve copies of only two turndowns. Finally Pascal Covici
accepted *Tortilla Flat*, and ever since he has been John Steinbeck's
publisher.

Steinbeck was puzzled, both before and after publication of *Tortilla
Flat* at the failure of critics and readers to distinguish his theme. "I
want to write something about *Tortilla Flat*," he told his agents in
March, 1934. "The book has a very definite theme. I thought it was
clear enough. I had expected that the plan of the Arthurian cycle
would be recognized. Even the incident of the Sangreal in the search
of the forest is not clear enough, I guess. The form is that of the
Malory version—the coming of Arthur, and the mystic quality of
owning a house, the forming of the Round Table, the adventures of
the knights and finally, the mystic translation of Danny. The main issue
was to present a little known and to me delightful people.

"Is not this cycle or story or theme enough? Perhaps it is not
enough because I have not made it clear enough. Then I must make it
clearer. What do you think of putting in an interlocutor, who between
each incident interprets the incident, morally, aesthetically, historically,
but in the manner of the paisanos themselves? This would give the
book much the appeal of the Gesta Romanorum, those outrageous
tales with monkish morals appended, or of the Song of Solomon in
the King James Version, with the delightful chapter headings which go
to prove that the Shulamite is in reality Christ's Church. It would not
be as sharp as this, of course. But the little dialogue would at least
make clear the form of the book, its tragi-comic theme, and the
different philosophic-moral system of these people.

"A cycle is there. You will remember that the association forms,
flowers and dies. Far from having a hard theme running through the
book, one of the intents is to show that rarely does anything in the
lives of these people survive the night."

Obviously, John Steinbeck as a writer was never quite the naive
primitive discovered by some of his hoity-toity critics.

Fortunately, Steinbeck gave up the plan for an interlocutor; and readers of *Tortilla Flat* took it to their hearts, with or without the Arthurian cycle. It was Steinbeck's first experience of success, and that bothered him. He had written *Tortilla Flat* more rapidly and easily than some of its predecessors, and he remarked to his agents, "Curious that this second-rate book, written for relaxation, should cause this fuss. People are actually taking it seriously."

He added, in a vein that ran like a motif through his letters of those years, "I am scared to death of popularity. It has ruined everyone I know. That's one of the reasons I should like *In Dubious Battle* printed next. Myths form early, and I want no tag of humorist pinned on me, nor any other kind."

He was leery of the conventional publishers' publicity. "I am never photographed," he told his agents. "This is not temperament on my part, nor is it self-consciousness. I do not believe in mixing personality with work. It is customary, I guess, but I should like to break the custom. A public nauseated with personal detail would probably be more grateful than otherwise . . . Please get this point over with enough force to make it stick for some time."

Steinbeck may have been wrong about the public's nausea with personal detail, but he stuck to his point. He was so convinced of it that, living out in California, he thought that even Alexander Woollcott must agree with him. After the Book-of-the-Month Club had taken *Of Mice and Men* and made Steinbeck a national figure, Woollcott asked for material he could use in a broadcast. The agents passed on the request to Steinbeck.

"I think you know my hatred of personal matter," he replied. "I hope you will get some of that impression over to Mr. Woollcott. On the other hand I should like to have him talk about the work. Factual material doesn't matter, but tell him, please no personalities. I simply can't write books if a consciousness of self is thrust on me. Must have my anonymity. . . . Unless I can stand in a crowd without self-consciousness and watch things from an uneditorialized point of view, I'm going to have a hell of a hard time. I'm sure Mr. Woollcott will understand this. I'm sure that of his own experience he will know the pressures exerted by publicity are unendurable."

Mr. Woollcott knew far more than Steinbeck about the pressures exerted by publicity, but he was not the man to find any of them unendurable; he lived for limelight. Steinbeck, unhappy about the ballyhoo over *Mice* in 1937, could not then dream what pressures would be exerted on him after *The Grapes of Wrath*. But he was right in his attitude; the writer who becomes a public personality inevitably loses something of his normal attitude to his fellow men. He becomes an Author with a capital A, set apart from common men. It seldom helps.

Still, the royalties from *Tortilla Flat* and the later, much larger, returns from *Of Mice and Men* changed the material conditions of Steinbeck's life. "Life has become very beautiful since I got a kerosene heater for my workroom," he wrote. "Completely changed attitude toward all kinds of things. Warm hands are fine."

Tortilla Flat was sold to the movies for $4000, which seemed big money to Steinbeck in those days, and on conventional terms which he later regretted. They gave him no control over changes made in the script. But in 1935 Steinbeck had not yet developed that passionate interest in dramatic forms and in the mass audience of the movies which was so powerfully to affect his career for the next decade. When a possible dramatization of *Tortilla Flat* was suggested in October, 1935, he instructed his agents to do as they thought best about it; he knew, he said, nothing of the process. When a movie contract was suggested, he again expressed indifference. "On an average," he wrote, "I go to about one movie a year."

"My stuff isn't picture material," he was still insisting in January, 1936. "If it is bought it is because of some attendant publicity. *Tortilla Flat* was the exception. There won't be a nibble on *In Dubious Battle* and if there were the producers would not use the story, and it is a conscientious piece of work. But there won't be anything lost. I'm not a popular writer in spite of the recent fluke."

In Dubious Battle was the first of three very different Steinbeck books dealing with the migratory farm laborers on the California fruit farms, and it was the bitterest of the three. "I guess it is a brutal book," he wrote when he was still at work on it, in February, 1935, "more brutal because there is no author's moral point of view. The speech of workingmen may seem a little bit racy to the ladies' clubs, but since ladies' clubs won't believe that such things go on anyway, it doesn't matter. I know this speech and I'm sick of workingmen being gelded of their natural expression until they talk with a fine Oxonian flavor. . . . A workingman bereft of his profanity is a silent man."

A New York editor in Pascal Covici's office read the manuscript of *In Dubious Battle* conscientiously and wrote a three-page single-space report indicating points at which Steinbeck's Communist organizer diverged from the orthodox party line as expressed by the ideologists of New York. Steinbeck took this letter as a rejection and almost went to another publisher, but when Mr. Covici discovered what his assistant had written he hastily assured Steinbeck that he was willing to publish the book if Steinbeck wished, though he was obviously somewhat alarmed at its violence.

"I would rather stay with Covici, Friede than with anyone I know," Steinbeck informed his agents. "I like the way they worked on *Tortilla Flat* and I like their make-up and everything about them. This letter this morning from them offers to publish *In Dubious Battle* if I wish it. Of course I wish it. It is a good book. I believe in it." As to the Communist ideology, he explained, "My information for this book came mostly from Irish and Italian Communists whose training was in the field not in the drawing-room. They don't believe in ideologies and ideal tactics. They do what they can under the circumstances."

The book was published as Steinbeck wrote it. Critics, not unnaturally, tended to discuss its politics. Steinbeck was irked. "So far," he complained to McIntosh and Otis, "Burton Rascoe and Ben Abramson are the only two reviewers who have discovered that *In Dubious Battle* is a novel and not a tract. Perhaps more will later."

Of Mice and Men was Steinbeck's first big success, and Steinbeck had had various troubles in writing it. "The microcosm is rather difficult to handle and apparently I did not get it over," he remarked when the book was in process—"the earth longings of a Lennie who was not to represent insanity at all but the inarticulate and powerful yearning of all men." Another time he spoke of the book as "an experiment in making a play that can be read or a novel that can be played . . . to find a new form that will take some of the technics of both." This was a problem that was to concern him for years.

By this time, of course, Steinbeck again had a dog, Toby, "a very serious dog who doesn't care for jokes." And Toby made trouble for

Mice. "Minor tragedy stalked," he wrote on May 27, 1936. "My setter
pup, left alone one night, made confetti of about half of my
manuscript book. Two months work to do over again. It set me back.
There was no other draft. I was pretty mad, but the poor little fellow
may have been acting critically. I didn't want to ruin a good dog for a
manuscript I'm not sure is good at all. He only got an ordinary
spanking." *Mice,* and critical enthusiasm began to boil, Steinbeck still
felt that Toby might have been right. "I'm not sure Toby didn't know
what he was doing when he ate the first draft," he wrote. "I have
promoted Toby-dog to be a lieutenant-colonel in charge of literature.
But as for the unpredictable literary enthusiasms of this country, I
have little faith in them."

He was already mulling over *The Grapes of Wrath,* and it was hard
going. "Having the devil's own time with this new book, but I am
enjoying it," he wrote in January, 1937. "The new book has struck a
bad snag," he said two weeks later. "Heaven knows how long it will
take me to write. The subject is so large that it scares me. And I am not
going to rush it. It must be worked out with care. That's one thing this
selection will do. It will let me work without a starvation scare going on
all the time. This may or may not be a good thing."

The success of *Of Mice and Men* made possible Steinbeck's first trip
to Europe. He sailed on a Swedish ship. He had always been
interested in the Scandinavian countries. Scandinavian translations of
Tortilla Flat were the only ones he had asked to see, explaining that
perhaps his interest was due to his fondness for Selma Lagerlöf's
Gösta Berling.

"This is a fine ship," he reported cheerfully from shipboard in May,
1937. His agents had sent him a "lovely bottle" as a bon voyage, and
he thanked them for it. "The day after we sailed we were invited to a
party in honor of the king and queen of Sweden. At least two thirds of
the people on board were Swedes. Well, we toasted the king and
queen in punch. We listened to stuffy speeches and gave a few
half-hearted gutteral cheers and we went to bed. Now there are only
two Norwegians on board. One at our table. He told us that the
seventeenth of May was the Norwegian Fourth of July, the day of
independence. Immediately we felt a surge of patriotism. Spiritually
we felt Norwegian. And your bottle was the nucleus. With only two

Norwegians, and we two as a kind of auxiliary Norwegians, we turned the ship into a fury. We made speeches. Wine, beer and brandy ran like water. All evening we toasted everything we could think of. Gradually the Swedes began to feel a certain love for Norway. At two this morning the riot was still going on. The Swedes are jealous but admiring. Even the two Norwegians don't know just how it happened. And your bottle of wine started it. I know you will be glad that your gift was the node of a new international brotherhood. I know you will. And I bet you never heard forty Scandinavians rise with their glasses in their hands and solemnly sing

'Sent Looisss Voomans, vit you diment errings

Chessed det men aroun de apron strings.'

It was unique in international feelings. It was very beautiful."

The Steinbecks returned from Europe sooner than they had planned. On September 12, Steinbeck wrote from Los Gatos, "So very glad to be home." He went back to work on *The Grapes of Wrath*.

He had written a series of articles on the migrant workers for the *San Francisco News* in October, 1936, before *Of Mice and Men* was published. He had worked on the farms of his long valley long ago in his school vacations. He knew the work; he knew the people. He knew the bitternesses. He felt them in the marrow of his bones. He also had a deep affectionate sense of identification with the fruit-pickers; and he was a Californian, and he felt a responsibility.

"I must go over into the interior valleys," he wrote Elizabeth Otis in the midst of reports on work in progress. "There are five thousand families starving to death over there, not just hungry but actually starving. The government is trying to feed them and get medical attention to them, with the Fascist group of utilities and banks and huge growers sabotaging the thing all along the line, and yelling for a balanced budget. In one tent there are twenty people quarantined for small pox and two of the women are to have babies in that tent this week. I've tied into the thing from the first and I must get down there and see it and see if I can do something to knock these murderers on the heads.

"Do you know what they're afraid of? They think that if these people are allowed to live in camps with proper sanitary facilities they will organize, and that is the bugbear of the large landowner and the corporation farmer. The states and counties will give them nothing because they are outsiders. But the crops of any part of this state could not be harvested without them. . . . Talk about Spanish children. The death of children by starvation in our valleys is simply staggering. . . . I'll do what I can. . . . Funny how mean and how little books become in the face of such tragedies."

He did what he could, and returned home to dash off a book that was announced under the title *L'Affaire Lettuceburg*. And when it was done he sat down and wrote a joint letter to his agent and his publisher, a letter beautifully and painfully illustrative of Steinbeck's attitude toward his own work: "Dear Elizabeth and Pat," he began. "This is going to be a hard letter to write. I feel badly about it. You see this book is finished and it is a bad book and I must get rid of it. It can't be printed. It is bad because it isn't honest. Oh! the incidents all happened but—I'm not telling as much of the truth about them as I know. In satire you have to restrict the picture and I just can't do satire. I've written three books now that were dishonest because they were less than the best I could do. One you never saw because I burned it the day I finished it. The second was the murder novel and this is the third. The first two were written under rather frantic financial pressure, and this last one from an obligation pressure I felt. I know, you could sell possibly 30,000 copies. I know that a great many people would think they liked this book. I, myself, have built up a hole-proof argument on how and why I liked it. I can't beat the argument, but I do not like the book. And I would be doing Pat a greater injury in letting him print it than I would be destroying it. Not once in the writing of it have I felt the curious warm pleasure that comes when work is going well. My whole work drive has been aimed at making people understand each other and then I deliberately write this book, the aim of which is to cause hatred through partial understanding. My father would have called it a smart-alec book. It was full of tricks to make people ridiculous. If I can't do better I have slipped badly. And that I won't admit—yet. . . ."

So he went back to the grind, plodding his way through *The Grapes of Wrath*. For a long time the book had no title. In September, 1938, the title went to New York on a postcard, followed by a letter saying that Steinbeck liked the title "because it is a march, because it is in our own revolutionary tradition and because in reference to this book it has a large meaning. And I like it because people know the Battle Hymn who don't know the Stars and Stripes."

That autumn he was on the home stretch. "I am desperately tired," he wrote, "but I want to finish. And mean. I feel as though shrapnel were bursting about my head. I only hope the book is some good. Can't tell yet at all. And I can't tell whether it is balanced. It is a slow plodding book but I don't think that it is dull." He also didn't think it would be a popular book.

It wasn't dull and it was popular. It made history in the publishing world and it changed history in the migrant camps of California. It was wildly praised and even more wildly denounced; what mattered was that it was read. But it left Steinbeck exhausted; it took months for him to recover from the long process of gestation. It was utterly impossible for him to do as he had often done before: to start work on a new book before the last was published. And the success of the book did to him some of the things he had feared success might do: "I'm so busy being a writer that I haven't time to write," he complained. "Ten thousand people have apparently put aside all other affairs to devote themselves to getting me to speak. And I'm so increasingly afraid in crowds that I do not talk comfortably to a pair of dice any more."

Moreover the war was looming on Steinbeck's, as on the world's, horizon, changing his course as it changed the world's. He tried for a time to escape in Mexico, first on the collecting expedition with Edward F. Ricketts which later bore fruit in *Sea of Cortez*, and subsequently in writing the script for the Mexican movie, *The Forgotten Village*. He took flying lessons, and was amazed to discover that "far from giving one a sense of power it gives one a sense of humility." He helped make pictures in Hollywood and out of Hollywood. But all this seemed secondary. "There's an imminence in the air as though anything not having to do with the war must be quickly done," he wrote in February, 1942. "If there is a London, I want to be in London this summer."

He liked writing *Sea of Cortez*. He had always been something of a biologist at heart, and very much of a craftsman. He had enjoyed the technique of novel-writing to a book about science. "Perhaps it is a little crazy," he explained, "but it is a good clearing-out of a lot of ideas that have been working on me for a long time and they do fit into the loose framework and design of such a book. . . . Pat is getting a darned fine book and one that he probably can't sell at all. It will be fun to read but not by the take-a-book-to-bed public. . . . The more I consider it the less very wide appeal it seems to me to have. The general public is not given to playful speculation. The rage and contempt of the critics will be amusing and like old times. It will be kind of good too because the work is pretty good. I know it is. It certainly is the most difficult work I've ever undertaken."

The war loomed ever larger. Steinbeck wanted to help, and various agencies of the government asked him to help. He responded eagerly to every opportunity—and was constantly frustrated, as so many others were, by the wide gap between enthusiasm at the top and the ruts of bureaucratic routine. *The Moon Is Down* actually grew out of a serious discussion with Colonel William J. Donovan of the Office of Strategic Services on techniques for aiding resistance movement in the occupied countries of German-held Europe. *Bombs Away* was the outgrowth of a series of suggestions made by General "Hap" Arnold of the Army Air Forces. But chasing about the United States of America in pursuit of material usable in wartime about the Army Air Forces was an occupation which involved considerable psychic frustration.

Steinbeck felt more at home when, early in 1943, he crossed to Europe in a convoy packed with soldiers, to do war reporting for the New York *Herald Tribune*. That was his own idea; he had shyly inquired whether the *Herald Tribune* would be interested in having him as a correspondent. He worked hard, and at first happily. The restraints of censorship eventually gnawed him, as they gnawed every correspondent. He did a good steady daily job; but when he came home, in October, 1943, he knew that his daily stories were not a book. For him a book was not just a collection of journalistic pieces; it had to have a life of its own; it took time to grow.

Yet so long as the war was on, it was impossible for John Steinbeck to settle down to sustained work on anything not connected with the war. His wartime letters are full of unfinished projects—war and non-war. All through the years, indeed, odd projects had been appearing in them, then disappearing, and usually reappearing. *Cannery Row*, however, came suddenly, late in 1944, without preparation in the letters—a nostalgic return to the moods of *Tortilla Flat* days, a "mixed-up book," as Steinbeck himself described it, with a "pretty general ribbing" in it.

A play referred to as *The Pipes* turns up in the letters occasionally, then fades away; various movie projects and temporary government jobs receive passing mention; there is a long saga of excitements and postponements concerned with the moving picture, *The Pearl of the World*, produced in Mexico in 1945, for which Steinbeck wrote a script that became a magazine story—"a strange piece of work," according to its author, "full of curious methods and figures. A folktale, I hope. A black-and-white story like a parable."

"I don't think I shall ever do another shooting script," he wrote in July, 1945. "It isn't my kind of work—this moving a camera around from place to place."

In the letters there is at first casual, then increasingly excited, talk of a book to be called *The Wayward Bus*—"it might be quite a book," Steinbeck thought in mid-1945, adding, "There is no hurry." There are also, of course, always references in the Steinbeck letters to the Steinbeck dogs—after 1943 to a huge blue-eyed English shepherd dog, Willie, and later to Steinbeck's son, whose advent changed Willie's nature. Willie, like his master, had been a bit of a rover, which sometimes complicated the pattern of Steinbeck family life. But after Tom appeared, when Willie could have had complete freedom, he didn't want it. Willie just wanted to stay at home and take care of the baby.

So there, in fifteen years of letters to an agent's office that became an author's permanent home, is the story of a creative writer at work. Certain patterns are recurrent: the restless wandering, when a story is in gestation; the false starts; then the utter absorption in creation, when the letters become sparser and the work is everything; finally, fatigue, uncertainty of the product, and a few wisps of anger at critics' misunderstanding. The war interrupts, but merely interrupts, the recurrent pattern; and now the war is over. The rest of the autobiography is for John Steinbeck—aided, of course, by Willie and by Tom and by Gwyn—to write, and it would be presumptuous for a critic to attempt to anticipate it. But there is a suggestive footnote which occurs in a letter written in the spring of 1945:—

"Ed Ricketts says that when he was little he was in trouble all the time until he suddenly realized that adults were crazy. Then, when he knew that, everything was all right and he could be nice to them. He says he has never found occasion to revise that opinion. Tom will probably be going through the same evaluation. And if he doesn't discover it for himself I will try to help him."

Interview with a Best-Selling Author: John Steinbeck

Robert van Gelder/1947

From *Cosmopolitan* (April 1947), pp. 18, 123-125. Reprinted with permission of *Cosmopolitan* magazine.

"Ideas," John Steinbeck remarked, "are like rabbits. You get a couple," he said, "and learn how to handle them, and pretty soon you have a dozen."

Steinbeck's voice is light and works as a barometer of his interest. It warms and speeds up when he is talking about people or things he likes. He spread out details from a fund of dramatic material that he has gathered on resistance tactics used against the Germans in Norway and Denmark. He's like to use this material in a couple of articles, he said. He told of how cocaine was sprinkled on the gangplanks of Danish fishing boats to deceive German bloodhounds when they were being brought aboard to sniff for hidden passengers. The dogs were temporarily useless after sniffing cocaine, but the Germans never found that out.

He told, too, of the high-ceilinged "parachute room" in a Norwegian prison. It was fitted with five tiers of bunks and the occupants of all the bunks had to jump to the floor and stand at attention whenever a German appeared. The men in the higher bunks were certain to break their legs sooner or later. This room is proudly displayed today as a kind of national monument.

Steinbeck talked freely of this project because he probably won't do anything about it. Of the play that he is writing he says only, "It's a new technique—for me. I'm fascinated by it."

There is not much quickening in his voice when he talks of work he has done in the past. Each of his books has represented to him a stage in his own growth and when the book is completed he feels he is through with that stage. "A good thing, too. I certainly don't want to write the same book over and over." He still has some interest in his new novel, *The Wayward Bus*, though he wouldn't talk much about it.

This is a tale concerning a branch-line bus driver, his wife, and a group of passengers. The scene is a valley in California, the time today, but I said that it seemed to me an allusive book, that I thought I had caught in it some echoes of *The Canterbury Tales*.

"Well sure," Steinbeck responded. "Chaucer, the *Heptaméron*, and Boccaccio's *Decameron*—it has an indefinite number of echoes of these. It is very carefully and elaborately built. Its architecture is—well—Gothic."

But when I started to discuss possible meanings of *The Wayward Bus* he cut me off.

"It isn't a light book, though it may read like one. Readers will find their own meanings in it, depending on what they bring to it. I think it is a good job—a lot of craftsmanship went into it. But I don't want to dig around in it."

He frequently mentions in his conversation the phrase, "the craft of writing." About one young writer he asked, "Is he man enough to learn his craft?" He spoke of his own difficulties in learning his craft. I asked him just what he meant by "the craft of writing."

He answered, "It is the art of penetrating other minds with the figures that are in your own mind." He feels that the human mind is a very complicated machine and that there are none too many entrances into it. In making his own entrances into other minds, he said, he puts trust in the sound of words, in a kind of lulling with syllables. Sound prepares the way for the impact of ideas. When he was young, Steinbeck was influenced by two writers, Donn Byrne, the author of *Messer Marco Polo*, and James Branch Cabell, whose best-known book is *Jurgen*. "The words didn't have to mean much," says Steinbeck. "These men were specialists in sound—and that's what I was after. When I'd get what they had to give I knew what I wanted to do."

Steinbeck writes his books in his head. he remarked that if he made notes he'd probably lose them anyway. He plans his stories even to the dialogue and when he starts writing he makes very fast progress, keeping up a pace of twenty-five hundred words each day.

His workplace now is in New York. Steinbeck is a native of California and used that state as the setting for most of his books—*The Long Valley, In Dubious Battle, Tortilla Flat, The Grapes of Wrath, Cannery Row, The Wayward Bus*. But recently he bought a pair of adjoining houses in New York's middle East Side. He rents one house to a friend and works and lives in the other with his wife and two small children.

The house has a fine atmosphere of peace and assurance. Steinbeck is quite proud of the kitchen. He likes to stand around in it and watch other people cook. He doesn't consider himself much of a cook although he's done a lot of it. He is much taken by his new washing machine. "It's the smartest thing in the house," he says. "I think we could hire it out as a baby watcher."

Of the living room he says, "It will be a fine place for a party—if we give any." But when he has work in progress, social life is held to a minimum. "No drinking, no going around. I live on a semi-automatic level and just work."

Steinbeck's workroom is in the basement. There are a couple of narrow vents cut into the walls to admit air but there is no window. "I don't need much air," Steinbeck said, "and a window kills me. I can find something to look at out of any window." On one wall there is an array of masks and on the other guns, fishing rods and an old dagger.

An electric typewriter stands in the center of the small room, but Steinbeck says he uses it only to write letters. He writes his manuscripts at a large desk in a very small hand. There is evidence of the usual writers' greed for various kinds of paper—yellow pads, stenographers' notebooks and bound manuscript books.

At one side of the desk there is an electric machine that records sound upon narrowly grooved plastic discs. One disc takes fifteen minutes of dictation on each side. Steinbeck reads from his manuscript into this machine, then plays the record back to get the sound of what he has written. He makes corrections, reads the corrected version onto fresh discs and sends the discs to his secretary for typing. *The Wayward Bus* filled forty-eight sides, twelve hours of playing time.

Steinbeck is now in his middle forties. He is fairly tall, with broad shoulders and a deep chest. He says that he is lazy.

He doesn't read many new books. He prefers to reread old ones: the diaries of Pepys and Evelyn, the WPA State Guides—of which the

Steinbecks have a complete collection—Gibbon's *The Decline and Fall of the Holy Roman Empire*. "I've never read the first volume of Gibbon's because it was missing from my set, but I've read the others several times."

He reads Hemingway and Faulkner and admires them very much. He enjoyed *Mr. Roberts*, by Thomas Heggen, and he talks enthusiastically of a neglected book by an English coal miner named Tom Hanlin. "The first chapter isn't good, but the rest of it is really excellent." He considers Bill Mauldin "a boy with great creative force."

"But who is doing new, experimental stuff?" he says. "Do you realize how much the feeling about writing has changed in, say, twenty years? When I was at the University (Stanford, in California) Sherwood Anderson's *Winesburg, Ohio*, was a stirring and shocking book—there was an enormous amount of emotion stirred up by it. The few of us who liked it were right back against the wall. I have a friend, Carl Wilhelmson, a Finn. When we were at school Carl had a rather thick accent. He liked the Anderson book. One day on the campus a whole group of students surrounded him and baited him about it. One girl was thoroughly angry—not putting on—angry. She shouted at Carl, 'What do you mean by liking that book? What is the purpose of that filth? What is the purpose of it?' Carl was excited too. 'What iss der purpose of art?' You could hear him a long way off. That's the way it was—exciting! Regular feuds. And what was that Fitzgerald book, the early one?"

"*This Side of Paradise.*"

"Yes. Well, there was a big row about that. But now, if such a book came along, there'd be no questions raised—a woman's magazine would publish it. I wonder what has happened to the excitement . . ."

He spoke several times of his luck in not being tempted, during the years when he was learning his craft, to write for a market with a middleman in the way.

"Have you ever heard a gang of three-thousand-dollar-a-week Hollywood writers cry?" he asked.

"As you see it, what do they cry about?" I asked.

"The misery of having to write a thing that is like some other thing because the other thing made money. There's no getting away from it—the investments are too big. So the writers are caught. They can't give up that Thursday pay check, so they just go along always doing as they're told to do. They all start the same way, take a good-paying job until they can save enough money to hit off on their own—but they never have enough, no matter what the pay check happens to be."

"And you weren't tempted?" I asked.

He shrugged. "No. I'm lucky. I had time to learn my craft. No one offered me a writing job."

Steinbeck made his way while he was learning to write with such jobs as that of winter caretaker for an estate near Emerald Bay, at Lake Tahoe, where he cut sixty cords of wood each winter for two years and wrote four novels, three of which he threw away. He worked as a laborer, from time to time, "at the kind of jobs that a semi-bum can get; damn tough work and poor pay."

"Did you ever write for money, just to hit a market?" I asked.

"Once. I wrote a detective story in nine days—we needed the money badly. Sixty thousand words in nine days. The trouble with it was that I satirized detective stories and my detective. I tried to use the formula and kid it at the same time. No one wanted it."

He said that when he was a carpenter's helper he couldn't saw boards straight. He toted plaster on a construction job and made a hundred dollars a week by working sixteen hours a day for a seven-day week. "That nearly killed me. When the whistle blew for lunchtime I'd drop the wheelbarrow handles and fall dead asleep."

His father eased his problem by giving him twenty-five dollars a month to live on while he wrote novels. "The first three novels I published didn't bring me in a thousand dollars altogether. The first didn't earn the $250 advance I'd been paid; the second earned about $400; and the third didn't earn its $250 advance."

"When did you become sure that you could keep on writing?" I asked.

"There was never any doubt about that," he said. "I was inured to semi-starvation and too lazy to get a regular job. I always knew that I'd keep on."

"It must have been easier after *Tortilla Flat*."

He said, "*Tortilla Flat* had good reviews, but the checks didn't start coming in until *Of Mice and Men*."

I asked him why he was in New York, away from the country and the people he knew best. He said New York is a perfect city in which to work; there is so much energy in the air. He mentioned the conveniences of metropolitan living.

He also likes New York, he says, because there you can keep good friends, yet not see them for months. "In a small community you must return invitations quickly or people wonder what made you sore. And in New York," he continued, "who is a celebrity? No one cares if you've written a book. The place is running over with people who write books. But," he adds, "New York is still a hick town." The people in his neighborhood ran a pool on the date when his wife would have her latest baby. A news dealer came closest to the time and won about $150.

"A pretty nice setup here," Steinbeck said. "Very nice for a time. But I have no illusions about literary success."

His voice put quotation marks around the phrase "literary success," and I felt that he was using it to mean "big sales" or "the big money."

"When it passes," he went on, "I know just where we'll head for—a warm country where coal is no problem and shelter is not much of a problem; near the sea, you can haul half the protein you need from the water; a little plot of arable land for vegetables. We'd like it,and the kids would love it. It would be adventure, another change, starting from scratch and building up. I won't mind that at all. You can get along, you know, without electric lights."

Country History: Writer to Chronicle Changes Since 1900

Jack Hollimon/1948

From *The Salinas Californian*, Rodeo Edition (June, 1948).
Reprinted with permission of *The Salinas Californian*.

John Steinbeck has returned to his home country for the material to be used in his newest novel, Monterey County. The well-known American author will bring half a century of Monterey county history to life as a backdrop for what is destined to be his lengthiest work.

Writer of works based on such widely diversified subjects as the German occupation of Norway (*The Moon Is Down*) to a technical study of marine life in the blue waters of the Pacific (*Sea of Cortez*) research journal written in collaboration with his lifelong friend, the late Ed Ricketts of the Pacific Grove Marine Laboratory, Steinbeck thus comes back to his native soil to, in his own words, ". . . write of my county, the place that I know best."

He was born Feb. 27, 1902 in Salinas, heart of the rich lettuce growing, cattle raising Salinas valley. He is the son of John Ernst Steinbeck, one-time county treasurer. The early years of Steinbeck's life were eventful ones in Salinas valley. He developed as the valley grew in population and agricultural production.

As a youth, he saw cattle and deer grazing in the valley between the Santa Lucia and Gabilian ranges, and witnessed the coming of irrigation that drove them into the foothills. He saw the gradual change over as the lettuce growers, the farmers and the intensified crop specialists spilled across the flatlands that formerly belonged to the tough cowmen and their stock.

His new novel will show the social eruption in this funnel-shaped stretch of land lying 100 miles south of San Francisco, walled by the mountain ranges and uprooted in the middle by the Salinas river bed. He plans to tell of the people, the land and the changes since the turn of the century.

"I intend to tell what happened," Steinbeck emphasized, "because I know this country best. Something has happened throughout the country since 1900. I am going to tell about those changes in the valley. As for why they came about, how can I or anyone else attempt to answer that?"

In a valley that has had families prosper and expand or wither and die through the vagaries of chance, Steinbeck has a fertile field for family characterization. He stoutly denies that any of the local families will be used as such in his novel.

As for plot, the new novel will have nothing to compare with what is usually diagnosed as "plot" by book critics. He merely wants to show the development of the people, chronicle events and record the changes in this newest of his creative efforts. "There will be no plot in the true sense of the word," he said. "It will be entirely different from my previous work."

Preparation going into the novel is shown in part by his arrangement with the *Salinas Californian*. Complete files of all editions dating back to 1900 are being turned over to Steinbeck for microfilming. He plans to read the papers for public reaction as put down day by day in the news accounts.

"Newspapers accurately recorded the lives of the people in the valley," he said. "I will obtain additional information by reading the editorials which mirrored their thinking." Steinbeck estimated at least six months will be spent in microfilming the papers, and at least a year will be devoted to their study. According to his work schedule, the book will be published sometime in 1950.

During his stay here recently, he used many hours driving over the back roads and through the outlying districts of the county to reacquaint himself with the topography and locations of landmarks. On one of these surveys, he drove east of Salinas to Natividad, thence over an almost forgotten stage road that crosses the Gabilans to San Juan Bautista, the largest Spanish Mission on the coast. Steinbeck walked the 18 miles as a boy, eating lunch halfway at a point where old cypress trees cast cooling shade on the dusty gravel trail.

He talks about the valley and what it has come to mean in the lives of so many people. He speaks of it as a woman, always using the feminine gender, and seems to convey the idea that "she is a woman capable of great evil."

"I cannot place my hand on it," he stated. "I do not know why I feel this evilness, but it is here—in the air, the trees and all about us."

Steinbeck's boyhood home in Salinas is still a proud place with fresh paint and sparkling clean windows. The architecture is Victorian, the scroll work ornamenting the eaves of the roof. There is a fence in the back that Steinbeck believes is the same one he constructed when he was here, although it has been many years since the Steinbecks moved and the house changed ownership.

Steinbeck is a big man. He stands well over six feet, and his features, nose, ears, and mouth are large. He shakes hands like an Italian fisherman off a Monterey purse seiner—a full, strong grasp that makes another man like and respect him. His eyes are magnetic. He seldom looks away, but instead is always watching you, boring into your inner thoughts. He has a "beartrap" mind—alert, intelligent, intellectual and cunning.

When he elects to answer, his words are direct and to the point. He recalls every phase of his work and can recount exact lines, phrases and words as they appear, indicating the effort that has gone into his writing. His well-tailored clothes fit him casually, the coat hanging loosely on his wide shoulders, his leanness and muscularness showing through.

After two months on the Pacific coast where he supervised the filming of his novel, *Cannery Row*, (the tale of the sardine packers and Doc, the philosophical marine specimen collector), Steinbeck crossed the country to his home in New York state to begin the arduous task he has cut out for himself on this latest and apparently most detailed undertaking. There will be a long wait but Steinbeck's own words make it worth waiting for—". . . I believe it will be my best."

Talk with John Steinbeck

Lewis Nichols/1952

Like many another man, outwardly upstanding, John Steinbeck
carries around with him a wide streak of self-confessed madness. In
his case, this takes the form of wanting to write plays. Since his normal
trade is that of being a serious novelist, it is only natural that the plays
to which he aspires would be comedies. This is inevitable, of course.
Whether or not it is Hamlet wanting to be the first gravedigger, Mr.
Steinbeck makes no secret of his ambition, although to date his
wooing of the theatre has been an oddly one-sided affair. He will fix
that up, some time. Or else.

This ambition, and certain other matters, Mr. Steinbeck explained
the other day, as *East of Eden* went into the bookstores. The other
matters ranged casually from formal research to an informal
exposition of what a well-trained myna bird should say. Of his latest
novel there was little, for Mr. Steinbeck is not one to gravely review his
work when there is anything else at hand. The word Art and its use of
the upper case would send him shuddering from the room. He is a
story teller with an antic imagination, and—together with his friend
and editor, Pascal Covici, as straight man—he probably would not
disgrace the Palace. An amiable man, he can eye his own personal
devil with amused detachment.

"I'm just determined I'm going to learn something about the
theatre," he said. "Last time we were kicked around like dogs
(*Burning Bright*, fifteen performances) but I still want to do it. This
shows a truly pure quality of stupidity. Just nuts. I'm so fascinated by
everything about the theatre, I don't really care if the show's a flop."

Now that *East of Eden* is out of his hands, Mr. Steinbeck will be free
to resume his interrupted courtship. He and Elia Kazan presently will
turn the novel into a script suitable for the screen, which is, after all, a

form of the theatre, if not the one to which Mr. Steinbeck currently aspires. More like it is talk of a Steinbeck-Frank Loesser collaboration on a musical version of *Cannery Row*. This is just talk so far, no more, but Mr. Steinbeck is eager. Anything to do with the theatre will find him running, like a fire buff after the engines.

But what about *East of Eden*? Was there nothing to say? Yes: the research had been agreeable.

"I went back through old Salinas (Calif.) newspapers," he began. "Wonderful things, those papers. Social notes, church notes, births, deaths. I finally got to the Boer War and found myself wondering who'd win." He stopped, then added moodily, "No matter how much checking you do, somebody's going to squawk about a mistake. And be right, too, likely.

"I saw some of the old timers. One of them bothered me. He said the thing he remembered about me was that one cold day I was walking along the street with my coat tied together with a horse blanket pin. That never happened. That was just making a good story. We weren't poor. Before being middle class became a phobia, we were proud of being it."

Lately returned from Europe, Mr. Steinbeck had in London a triumph he clearly regards in much the same light as a far lesser man would regard the Pulitzer Prize—he was invited to inspect the plumbing at Buckingham Palace. This came about through his indulgence in a passion which almost as strong as that for the theatre, a love of hardware stores. About this, there is some dispute. Mr. Steinbeck says he buys in hardware stores only those things he will actually use—"mostly"; Mr. Covici says, reprovingly, that he buys gadgets. At any event, a day after Mr. Steinbeck had indulged his craving during a long tour of British hardware, the ironworkers' guild telephoned and formally invited him on a tour below stairs at Buckingham. He will regret forever that he was unable to accept.

He now lives officially in New York, owning a house with a garden ("Just keep away from white flowers and a New York garden's easy") and a third floor room of his own. This, he says, is the first room of his own he ever has had. Machinery of one sort or another crowds all but one small corner, where is placed the hot seat for literary endeavor. Sawdust from woodworking instruments lies thick on the floor, and when the master is in residence, a glum sign on the door proclaims, "Buzzard's Despair." When he goes out, he meets on his return the reverse of the sign, "Tidy Town," which shows that women have got in and tidied up the place.

It is a very quiet room. For companionship, Mr. Steinbeck would like to get a myna bird. With a tape recorder he would teach this to ask questions, never answer, just ask. "Is that your wife with you?" "What are you doing here?" "Not looking so well today, are you, old man?" A quiet room where nothing ever happens.

Interview at a Barbeque: Writing Gets Harder as You Grow Older, Says Steinbeck

Charles Mercer/1953

From *The Oakland Tribune* 18 October 1953. Reprinted with permission of The Associated Press.

What manner of man is John Steinbeck, who writes such deeply etched characterizations as Lennie, in "Of Mice and Men"? A man with a figurative bottle of acid in his hand? You may be surprised at this look into his own backyard.

NEW YORK, 17 Oct.—(AP)—John Steinbeck, the writer, was grilling spareribs in his backyard after a hard day's work. At least he was supposed to be. Actually he'd sprawled out in a canvas chair and was reading a newspaper.

Steinbeck, as you probably know, is one of America's leading writers. "One of" means that you think of Ernest Hemingway, William Faulkner, John Steinbeck—and then you get into arguments depending on how your taste runs in literature.

If you've never met Steinbeck before, you naturally wonder what sort of man can draw the earth portraits which have characterized his best known writings: *The Grapes of Wrath, Tortilla Flat, Of Mice and Men, The Wayward Bus.* And you may not be prepared for what you find.

Steinbeck is 51 years old. He lives with his pretty, brown-haired wife and their two sons, Tom, 9, and John, 7, in a modernized four-story house on East 72nd Street. Behind the house is a space about 20 by 40 feet which passes in Manhattan as a back yard or a garden, depending on your income.

In the Steinbecks' yard is a riot of what they call Brooklyn trees, a hardy variety that thrives on concrete. They've planted shrubs and Steinbeck has spread gravel and set up an outdoor grill so that it's as

55

pleasant a spot as you could find in Manhattan on an Indian summer evening.

Steinbeck was wearing an old pair of pants and moccasins. He's a powerfully-built man with surprisingly little fat considering that he earns his living sitting at a typewriter. His hair is thinning. One feature that never comes through in photographs is his eyes. They're bright blue.

His son, John, was sitting in a chair next to his father's, talking his head off. Mrs. Steinbeck, who was working around the kitchen in shorts, brought us cans of beer and reminded him to turn the spareribs. Steinbeck was trying to open the beer and get to the grill and be pleasant to a visitor and patiently answer John's questions when down through the trees overhead came the very unmusical notes of a toy flute.

The voice of an invisible boy cried from an upper window of the house, "Hey, Pop, I can't play this thing."

"Keep trying, Tom, keep trying," Steinbeck called back.

He strolled to the grill, an oil drum cut lengthwise, and opened by a pulley so that it looked like an enormous pair of jaws.

Over a bed of charcoal were three big lengths of spareribs and six huge potatoes wrapped in aluminum foil. I remarked I'd never seen an oil drum converted into a grill before.

"Pop," said John, "What's an oil drum?"

"An oil drum," Steinbeck said slowly, "is—it's a drum that holds oil."

"Oh," John said dubiously.

The unmusical notes of the flute drew near as Tom strode into the yard accompanied by two spaniels.

Steinbeck brushed the meat with barbecue sauce. The juvenile clamor was deafening.

"Hey, scram!" he said suddenly to the boys. "Beat it, both of you. This is the parents' hour."

They scrammed cheerfully, their egos obviously undamaged by parental authority.

Steinbeck has nearly finished a short novel tentatively entitled "The Bear Flag," which probably will be made into a Broadway musical.

"I write better in New York," he said, "because there are too many distractions in the country—too many things I want to do. I write from about 10 to 5 on the top floor of the house and I always write 2000 words a day. Sometimes I run as high as 3000, but the last thousand usually aren't as good.

"I start out to write five days a week, and then it runs to six days and finally seven. Then, eventually, that wave of weariness overwhelms me and I don't know what's the matter. That is, I know but I won't admit it. I'm just tired from writing.

"As you get older, writing becomes harder. By that I mean you see so many more potentialities. Things like transition used to trouble me. But not any more. When I say it's harder, I'm not talking about facility. You learn all the so-called tricks, but then you don't want to use them."

What about his most recent novel, *East of Eden*, in which Steinbeck wanders in and out as a first person narrator? Is that an illustration of what he means?

"That's right. I don't mean I consciously set out to break down an established novel form. It just occurred to me that the author has become so absent from the modern novel, he's so careful never to get into the act, that it's actually become a stereotype. I felt I could tell *East of Eden* better by being in it myself, so I went back to the days of Fielding, (the 18th Century novelist) and told it that way.

"I don't rewrite so much. I find I have more of a tendency to overwrite, to use two or three words where one will do it better. I have to go back and cut and cut."

Steinbeck didn't rattle this off the way it's set down here. He speaks slowly, almost reluctantly. He examines a question and its motive reflectively. He wandered off frequently to turn the spareribs; probably in most conversations he tends some figurative spareribs while mulling the passage of words.

Some people who know him slightly say he's shy. It doesn't appear so. It seems rather the innate modesty often found in the ablest of writers, artists and scientists. This sort of individual, absorbed in ideas and methods, prefers to let a finished work speak for him. Steinbeck is profoundly skeptical of the flat generalization.

I tested him on a few:

Advice to young writers—"Just keep writing. But I didn't say that. Everybody's been saying that for years."

His own view of his place in American letters—"Oh, Lord! I never have the time or inclination to read a book over once it's published. You know how it is."

His favorite contemporary writers—"I enjoy reading a lot of them."
    After a while we both grew embarrassed by my attempts to write a
headline for a story. I apologized for trying to make him utter a cliche.
    "That's okay," he said gently and smiled.
    "The world lives by cliches. So do I. I just don't seem able to think
of a good one this evening."

John Steinbeck:
The Sphinx Talks
Sidney Fields/1955

From *The New York Sunday Mirror* 13 March 1955.

It was all nonsense, the notions heard about John Steinbeck being a sphinx and disliking interviews. He's friendly, and even eager to tilt a verbal lance or two with any comer about anything: The uneasy world; writing and writers; movies; his sons Tom, 10, and John, 8; or the presents he got on his 53rd birthday last Feb. 27. One of them was a 17th century crossbow from Cy Feuer and Ernie Martin, who told Steinbeck:

"You're probably the only man in New York who would say: 'This is just exactly what I needed.'"

Steinbeck likes the feel and thought of old things. Maybe because anything old can tell us something new. He's a huge man, with blue, restless eyes. He writes with a razor as well as compassion, and talks the same way. His wife says of his voice: "It's a nice one. It says good things." He writes novels, but avoids reading fiction, preferring books on biology, physics, philosophy, and comic strips.

"Yes, comic strips," he says. "I read them avidly. Especially Li'l Abner. Al Capp is a great social satirist. Comic strips might be the real literature of our time. We'll never know what our literature is until we're gone. But more people read comic strips than books or anything else."

His novel *East of Eden* has been made into a movie, and is now at the Astor. Steinbeck likes the movie version because of its tightness, its unity, because it grabs an audience and shakes it, like a terrier shaking a squirrel.

"I've been lucky," he says. "A lot of my books have been made into movies, and the best movies were the ones I had nothing to do with."

Another of his books, *Sweet Thursday*, will be shown as a Rodgers and Hammerstein musical this Fall, and he's delighted with Hammerstein's book and lyrics, and Rodgers' music.

"Dick Rodgers asked how I liked Hammerstein's book and lyrics," Steinbeck says, "and when I told him I loved them, Dick said: 'I can't wait to hear the music.'"

Presently Steinbeck is formulating a novel about the uneasy people trying to escape the uneasy world through science fiction. The H-bomb could settle their fears, but while they await it they still have to struggle with the sense of order that's gone.

"Life is just all speculation, isn't it?" Steinbeck says. "And the pressure of population is explosive. Before there was a way out. Wars and pestilence. The Thirty Years' War took two thirds of Europe. The war in Korea took less than half of one percent of the soldiers and civilians. We've licked pestilence. We're even licking old age . . . Say, am I pontificating?"

No! No! Go on, please.

"There's the story about the doctors in a home for the aged feeding their patients compressed liver. It took them out of bed and put them on the croquet courts, and all hell broke loose. You can see what that would do to the population of the world."

He and his wife have been reading deeply about the origins of faith and Christianity. They're certain the uneasy world is hungering for a new Mithras or the second coming of Christ.

"By giving the soul of man importance," says Steinbeck, "Jesus created the first big human revolution. The second might be the liberation of the human mind from its fear."

Steinbeck is from Salinas, Calif., where his father was county treasurer. His mother was a schoolteacher. At Stanford University he studied only what he wanted to, and in between knocked about America, working on cattle and fruit ranches, a sugar refinery, a trout hatchery. He carried the bricks that built Madison Square Garden, and was a New York newspaper reporter, but was fired because he was less interested in the story than the hopes and poetry of the people involved.

He couldn't sell his first three novels. His next three sold less than 3,000 copies. His first published book, *Cup of Gold*, was written while he worked as Winter caretaker of an estate. For a while he lived on

$25 a month; his food was mostly the fish he caught. After *Tortilla Flat* he began gaining acceptance. In 1940 he won the Pulitzer Prize with *The Grapes of Wrath*.

He lives in New York because "once you've been here no other city is good enough." But it still frightens him. When his first son was born he was in an East Side flat, and was certain no one knew or cared if he was there.

"But when Tommy came we found out there was a $300 neighborhood pool on the exact hour of his birth," Steinbeck says. "It was won by a newsdealer."

His present wife is his third. His sons are of his second marriage. They live near him, and his cellar is full of the play and dreams they share with their father. Steinbeck is a fiercely independent man, much alone with his thoughts. But his sons are centered in him. It's not possible to be an indifferent father and a good writer.

"They're both nuts about the water," he says, "and I'm trying to buy a little place near the shore in Sag Harbor."

When John, the eight-year-old found out about the plan, he demanded: "Pop, you just got to tell me you bought it." And when Steinbeck asked: "Why?" John said, "Because I can dream about it."

John Steinbeck Turns His Hand to Tale of Space Ship, Flying Saucers
Art Buchwald/1955

From *The International Herald Tribune* 29 March 1955.
Reprinted with permission of the author.

PARIS, 29 March.—Mr. John Steinbeck is writing a book about flying saucers. We found this out the other day just before leaving New York when we called him and asked if he had any tidbits he could spare for the column.

"Why," he said, "don't you columnists write your own articles? Every time I get a good idea you print it and then I don't have anything to write about."

"Mr. Steinbeck, may I remind you that if it wasn't for columnists there wouldn't be people? Any columnist will tell you he invented people. And he would be right in saying so. What exactly are you working on?"

"A flying saucer story."

"Please, Mr. Steinbeck, don't be vague."

"It's about a fellow in a small American town who is building a space ship. I am not interested in the space ship as much as I am in the people's attitude toward it. The town's divided between those people who are for him and those people who are against him."

"Is that an important theme?"

"Of course it's important. People are beating their brains against a new frontier. They've run out of terrestrial frontiers and they're heading out into space."

"What's your attitude toward space ships?"

"I have no attitude toward space ships. I only have an attitude toward people who have an attitude toward them."

"I get it. The guy builds a space ship and everyone tells him it won't fly and it does fly and the guy gets to Mars and no one laughs at him any more."

"You write your version," Mr. Steinbeck said, "and I'll write mine."

"Is there anything else you'd like to tell me, Mr. Steinbeck? I just put another dime in the telephone."

"If you really want a story I'll give you one. I'm changing my style. I'm tired of my own technique. I'm experimenting with something new. When a writer starts learning his craft everything is difficult and everything is fresh. Once he develops the technique, the technique starts choosing his subject matter. Pretty soon you know how to trick your audience. You no longer are master of your own work. In the case of the space ship story, I'm eliminating all the props of the novel. There is no description, no props. I'm dealing with nothing but dialogue.

"I feel as if I'm learning to write all over again. I don't mind admitting I've been highly discontented with my own work for some time. In *East of Eden* I used all my tricks and used them consciously and with finality. I've been thinking about this for three years. I discovered I had become a novelist when I should have stayed a writer.

"The novel isn't dead, but it's dead for me. I'm not abandoning the novel forever. Maybe I'll go back to it, but I'll be purified. Since I had this change of heart I feel like a new man. I'm alive again. A creative person has to be alive. He can't borrow from things he's done in the past. He can't let his method choose his subjects or his characters. They can't be warped to fit his style. That's why I'm taking on something entirely new.

"I've learned a great deal since I decided to experiment. I listen to people again. I discovered the way people talk. They don't talk as they're portrayed in many books—in clipped sentences, and in question-and-answer paragraphs. The way people really talk is one person grabs the conversation, holds it as long as he can."

"Are you afraid of the book critics in experimenting with your new method?"

"I don't care about the critics. The only joy for the writer should be the doing, not the end. Reception of a work should not be a part of the pleasure of writing. There is no creative satisfaction when a thing is finished. The thing I want to learn to do is write as freshly as when I first started. A writer should never learn to write. He must continually experiment or his technique will take over and he'll never write anything good again."

"That's pretty interesting, Mr. Steinbeck. I appreciate your giving it to me."

"That's all right. I was going to write it for the 'Saturday Review'."

"Well, you don't have to write it now. Keep this up and your debt to columnists will be paid in no time."

Healthy Anger
Books and Bookmen/1958

Books and Bookmen, England (October, 1958). Reprinted by permission.

These are the impromptu answers given by John Steinbeck to questions put to him by Diana, Lady Avebury, Public Relations for the Heinemann Publishing Group, in a filmed interview produced and directed by Heinemann for Australian Television.

Mr. Steinbeck, you were foreign correspondent in London during the war, and I understand that the dispatches you wrote will be published next year. Did you find it very difficult to remember what we were like in London then?

Not only what you were like, but what I was like. I hadn't seen the dispatches for—what is it, fifteen years since the end of the war? And when I read them, I realised there were so many things I didn't remember, and it seemed good that it should be re-published because there may be many other people who don't remember what *they* felt, what *they* saw and what *they* heard at the time.

Yes, life has changed a great deal since then, and I must confess I wondered if you had when I heard you'd been to Ascot—did you enjoy it?

I was dressed in rented clothing, sheeps clothing, and I'd been through the Moss Bros. routine and it was a period piece; you know, I've never seen anything quite like it—it was rather remarkable. I was dressed in the Moss Bros. uniform and felt a little ridiculous until I realised everybody else was exactly the same, and then it made me realise that Cecil Beaton did not invent the scene in *My Fair Lady*—there they were smelling of moth balls.

Did you have any luck?

Yes, we did, but it was more moral luck than anything else. You see my wife was forty-four, she was born on the 14th August at 4:40 in the afternoon in 1914. This was a sign from the heavens—when we

left, a neighbour of ours gave us £5 to invest on No. 4, and we decided to compound it by betting on the fourth race.

Well?

(At this point the interview, which had taken place in the garden,
was interrupted by a sudden outburst of rain.)

Please, Mr. Steinbeck, don't tell us what you think of our English
weather.

(John Steinbeck and his interviewer beat a hasty retreat into the
house.)

There is something else I would like to ask you, Mr. Steinbeck.

Will you let me finish that story because I'm going to eat on it for
quite a long time, and I think it's a good story. The only error in
judgment was that we bet No. 4 on the nose—if we'd bet him to come
in fourth we'd be very rich now because that's where he came in!

(Laughs). Mr. Steinbeck, you sound like an "angry young man."

Well, I was, and sometimes maybe I still am.

Then you approve of the angry young men?

Oh, surely. I think any young man or any man who isn't angry at
one time or another is a waste of time. No, no. Anger is a symbol of
thought and evaluation and reaction: without it what have we got? I'm
tired of non-angry people. I think anger is the healthiest thing in the
world.

James Dean symbolised the angry young man for a lot of people.

Yes, but there's one thing I deplore a little bit. James Dean
symbolises the angry young man against, but not towards something.
He's against things, but not *for* things.

He seems to symbolise a sort of death wish for a great many
people?

I never knew him so I don't know about that, but I noticed that the
symbol was that he was *against* instead of *for*.

And were you pleased with his performance in your film of the
book *East of Eden*?

Oh, yes. I thought he was a tremendously talented actor, and, of
course, he had an enormously talented director; I was very
fortunate in this film because I didn't see it made. I was not part of
it, and when I saw it, I saw it whole and I was deeply impressed
with it.

Have you, on the whole been pleased with the film treatment of your books?

That's very interesting. I've had some dogs, of course, but on the whole I've been very fortunate. I've had excellent people—Nunally Johnson and Jack Ford in *The Grapes of Wrath*, Lewis Milestone and Burgess Meredith in *Of Mice and Men*, and Elia Kazan and Jimmy Dean in *East of Eden*. I have no complaints—I think it is better than most people deserve. There is *one* thing that has occurred to me—Films and Books—a man reads a book and he makes his own pictures. If he reads the book first he resents the picture because it's not the picture he's made in his mind. Maybe it would be better if books and pictures didn't cross, and the person reading the book didn't see the picture and the person seeing the picture didn't read the book. Maybe that would be better.

Well, I see your point. Have you written for films?

Yes, I have, and I must say it isn't that I don't like it—I don't do it very well. You see my trade is very fortunate. I need only a five cent pencil and a pad of paper and I'm in business—I don't need producers, cameras, film, difficulties—it's a lovely profession. It needs no factory.

Now we've talked about films, let's get back to books—your profession.

Well, some people have called it a profession—some people have called it a trade, and some people have called it a perversion.

How do you start writing a book?

I haven't the slightest idea, so it will take quite a long time to tell you.

Have you a method?

Yes, I go to work every morning at 8:30 and stay there until I do a certain word rate.

It used to be more than it is now. It once was three thousand, and I found that I got tired—tired beyond tiredness. I try to keep it down now, but sometimes I get so excited I can't keep it down. I try to keep it down to about two thousand to fifteen hundred.

I write in longhand and then I read on tape and listen back.

Why tape?

Well, I've tried reading aloud but then my eyes are involved. I read on tape and listen back for corrections, because you can hear the

most terrible things you've done if you hear it clear back on tape. I do
it particularly with dialogue because then I can find whether it sounds
like speech or not.

Perhaps this is the explanation of your really superb dialogue.

Well, people don't talk like speech.

Mr. Steinbeck—you've been associated with a certain kind of
writing. How do you explain your last book to be published over here,
The Short Reign of Pippin IV?

I wish I could explain it, and I will try. It was a thing that came to me
in the night. I was working on something else. I tried to avoid it, I tried
to push it out and it interfered with my work, and I finally thought it
would be better to write it as a short story to get rid of it, and it turned
out to be 60,000 words—Pippin was an accident.

I think it was a brilliantly witty accident and I'm only surprised it
isn't a matter of French history already!

(John Steinbeck shrugged his shoulders in a typically French
manner.)

I've just been reading your *Log from the Sea of Cortez* and can't
tell you how moved I was by your biography of Ed Ricketts—the
original Doc of *Cannery Row.*

Well, I'm glad you were moved—I was destroyed. He was my
partner for eighteen years—he was part of my brain. At one time a
very eminent zoologist said that the two of us together were the best
zoologists in America, and when he was killed I was destroyed.

John Steinbeck Back — But Not to Stay

Mike Thomas/1960

From *The Monterey Peninsula Herald*, 4 November 1960.
Reprinted with permission of *The Monterey Peninsula Herald*.

"You can't go home again."

John Steinbeck, quoting Thomas Wolfe, was talking about himself.

We'd found him at home—his old home—in Pacific Grove. A couple of us, one an old friend and the other a youngish hero worshipper, had heard he was in town and dropped in at the old family place where his sister, Beth Ainsworth, lives now.

We found him repairing the old wooden front gate. There were bits of leaves in his thin, graying hair. He was wearing corduroy pants and a shapeless green shirt, and had a hatchet in one hand and a small pinch bar in the other.

"I haven't got the right tools," he grinned. "That's always my excuse."

He surveyed the gate, leaning slantwise against one post, and the scars on the other post, where he'd wrenched a hinge loose.

"It won't stay on and it won't come off," he said. "That's the way I make things."

"Did you build it yourself?" one of us asked.

"I must have," he said.

A small boy with a toy rifle and a very dirty face was fidgeting about the sidewalk. He was jabbering at Steinbeck and snapping his rifle at an aging poodle sitting in a car at the curbside.

Steinbeck looked at the nervous dog and scowled at the boy. He is a big man with a massive head and broad features. He wears a short, grayish goatee. Scowling he looked like a mildly annoyed lion.

In a deep growl, he intoned ominously:

"In Xanadu did Kubla Khan a stately pleasure-dome decree . . ."

The boy looked only faintly interested. Steinbeck shrugged and led us into the garden.

"I should have said buttered toast," he said. "That's what we used to say in Africa when the kids bothered us. We'd yell buttered toast and they'd run like the devil. They're frightening words, buttered toast."

We greeted Mrs. Ainsworth, Mrs. Mary Dekker of Carmel, Steinbeck's other sister, and Elaine, his wife. The ladies went back into the house and we settled down in wicker chairs with Mrs. Ainsworth's coffee.

"I've always loved this garden," said Steinbeck.

One of us asked him what he's working on now.

"I've just finished a very long novel," he said. "It started out to be a short novel, but—"

"What's it about?"

"Morals."

He said the new book, which will be published in the next few months, will be called *The Winter of Our Discontent*.

"It's from *Richard the Third*. The first line," he said. He quoted a bit of Shakespeare.

When he finished the book, he said, he and his wife left New York in a camper-body truck and made a slow trip west through the northern states. They got to the Monterey Peninsula two or three days ago. When they leave the middle of next week, they plan to take a slow trip back east, by the southern route.

Steinbeck's making the trip to renew his acquaintance with the country.

"I haven't been back here for—it must be twenty years," he said. "I've been writing from memory."

The conversation went on to other topics. As he talked, Steinbeck cocked his head forward, so that his fiercely blue eyes glittered from beneath shaggy brows. Now and then he took a cigarette in big, nicotine-stained fingers and ignited it with a lighter hanging from a string around his neck.

His voice is a rumble, so deep that each vibration is distinct. His frequent laughter comes from the depths and spreads all over.

One of us mentioned a magazine piece Steinbeck did recently about the 1930s. He said that for some unknown reason people seem to be interested in that period right now.

That was the time when Steinbeck was living here and writing the books that made Monterey famous, and Steinbeck considerably more so.

"There was something about that time," he said. "People seemed to be friendlier. Maybe it's because people are more inclined to help each other in hard times. Good times don't bring out the best in people.

"I remember when I sold my first story for ninety dollars," he said. "I thought the publishers were being outrageously extravagant. I got Toby Street and we bought a gallon of twenty-eight-cent wine. That was the one with the flies in it. And we still had eighty-nine dollars and seventy-two cents left."

There was more reminiscing, and one of us asked Steinbeck if he thought he'd ever come back to the Monterey Peninsula to live. He bowed his head, thought for a second, and said, "No."

"Tom Wolfe said it the best way," he said: "'You can't go home again.'

"I don't know anybody here anymore. Not many people, anyway. I used to walk down the street and know everybody I met. Now I'm a stranger.

"You don't go to a place for scenery. You go for people.

"I don't have a home. New York isn't a home, either. Elaine and I hear a boat whistle on the East River and we want to go."

But, he said, there's a strange thing about that. His two sons, both born and brought up "sitting on a fire hydrant, watching the traffic" in New York, feel a strong identification with the Peninsula and want to live here. One of his sons, Tom, came to Pacific Grove last year and is now a student at Pacific Grove High School.

Maybe, one of us suggested, if a person hasn't had deep roots in a place, as Steinbeck had in the Peninsula, he feels a need for roots and tries to find them.

"If you haven't had them," Steinbeck said. "If you've had them, you don't need them."

Later, when we moved into the house, one of us sank into an old rocking chair.

"Mother used to rock us in that chair," said Steinbeck.

As we were leaving, he picked up his tools and went back to repairing the old front gate.

John Steinbeck:
America's King Arthur Is Coming
Curt Gentry/1960

John Steinbeck, California's greatest novelist, was back in San Francisco last week. Not to come home again, just passing through, on the last lap of a cross country drive "to see how the people feel about the election."

Now 58, Steinbeck is big in body, mind and heart, as full of humor, vitriol, compassion, and strong feeling as his largest novel. Some 22 books ago, he spent his "attic days" in San Francisco, working at such jobs as hauling jute on the docks and writing. But he looked back for only a moment. Mostly he talked about the present—with strong comments on such diverse subjects as President Eisenhower, Vice President Nixon, Ernest Hemingway, his own forthcoming novel, and immorality.

"In the Twenties and Thirties it was a crime to be poor anywhere, except in Europe or San Francisco," he recalled. "Here it was mostly fun. If you had clean fingernails, a little spit polish on your shoes, and four silver dollars in your pocket you could have a wonderful time . . ." There were other times too.

He also remembered the day when George West, of the San Francisco News, said: "There are a bunch of people over in the valley starving, John. Do you want to go over and see what it is all about?" He went, to become totally involved with the plight of the migratory workers, his articles becoming the basis for his best-known novel, *The Grapes of Wrath*.

But mostly he talked about the present.

"A woman journalist in England asked me why Americans usually wrote about their childhood and a past that happened only in imagination, why they never wrote about the present. This bothered me until I realized why—that a novelist wants to know how it comes

73

out, that he can't be omnipotent writing a book about the present, particularly this one."

Nevertheless he decided to try. The result was *The Winter of Our Discontent*, which Viking Press will publish early next year.

"I started on Easter, 1960, intending to make it 60,000 words; I finished with 150,000 on July 9." Contemporary? "The action runs from Easter through July, the day before I finished it. That must be a first of some kind."

Its subject? "Immorality," which Steinbeck defines as "taking out more than you are willing to put in."

"A nation or a group or an individual cannot survive being soft, comforted, content. The individual only survives well when the pressure is on him. The American people are losing their ability to be themselves, to put back in. When people or animals lose their versatility they become extinct."

"People are not basically immoral," he went on. "They want to be moral but it takes a little courage, properly channeled. Take Hemingway and bullfighting . . .

"The Hemingway hero is so brave in the ring but outside it he doesn't have the guts to come out against Franco . . . Personally I love bullfighting. It's beautiful, with dignity, like a group of children at play. But what do you have at the end of the afternoon? Four dead bulls. You should have something more than that after a day of nobility . . . My God, what a writer!" he exclaimed, brandishing his walking stick. "I only wish he would be more an author of people: bullfighting is not good enough for him."

The next topic was not politics, as expected, but his long awaited Arthurian cycle. Since boyhood Steinbeck has been fascinated with the tales of King Arthur and his knights. They provided the framework for his first successful novel, *Tortilla Flat*, published in 1935. In recent years he has learned medieval Latin, Old French, and Anglo-Saxon while working on a translation of all of the tales, many of which have never before been translated because of their sexual explicitness. *The Winter of Our Discontent* was a breather from this favorite project.

"The American Western is the Arthurian cycle," he observed. "The King is the man who solves everything with a gun. The Western has its Guinevere and Gawain, all the characters. Arthur did not originate in

England; all people have their Arthur, and need him. He is created out of a need, when they are in trouble. America's Arthur is coming because the people need him."

This did lead into politics, on which subject Steinbeck admits happily that he is strongly partisan. He wouldn't be otherwise. He does not like people who do not believe in anything, who have no opinions, or having them are afraid to voice them. His angriest comment on the present Administration was that "they have made it socially fashionable to be stupid!"

"People are even afraid to admit that they read," he declared. "Here's an interesting thing: a first edition of one of my books is published in the same number of copies in Denmark, with a population of 5 million as in the United States with a population of 130 million . . ."

Steinbeck is an ardent and veteran Democrat.

The outcome of the election? Everywhere Steinbeck traveled he observed not apathy but great interest. The most important single event in the campaign, he believes is the *New York Times* endorsement of John Kennedy. "Suddenly all over the East it's again respectable to vote for a Democrat." He agrees with the commentator who said that few voters are undecided, they just refuse to commit themselves. "It will be a great secret vote," Steinbeck predicted, "close in the popular vote, a landslide in the electoral vote, with the winner taking every state except possibly two . . ."

And the winner? He wouldn't venture a guess.

John Steinbeck Says Changes Put World in Shock

Hal Boyle/1961

Reprinted with permission of The Associated Press.

NEW YORK—AP—"The whole world is in a state of shock," said author John Steinbeck. "That is why people don't think.

"You can't think when you're in a state of shock."

At 59 Steinbeck, rated among the best of the United States living writers, has turned out 27 books. His latest novel, *The Winter of Our Discontent*, will be published next month.

But for 30 years Steinbeck also has made an intensive study of the Middle Ages, and feels mankind is again entering that kind of historical period.

"Again we're seeing the breakup of old forms of authority— religious, governmental, even parental—before new ones are established," he said, puffing cheerfully on a pipe in the study of his east side home.

"That's why people are so restless and worried. They don't know what to tie to.

"There's even a new trend in cocktail parties here. Instead of showing up with their husbands or wives or mistresses or lovers, people bring their psychiatrists.

"Good Lord, the way we live."

But Steinbeck, who saw life in the raw in half a dozen jobs ranging from brick laying to war reporting, retains a wonderful gusto for living.

Rumpling his graying hair and beard, swiveling his glasses from his nose to the top of his head, he scribbles out 2,000 words of prose almost daily with a ball point pen in a series of old fashioned ledgers.

"I used to write 3,000 words a day, but it got to be too exhausting," he said.

The ledgers in which he writes would be gold mines to future literary scholars—if Steinbeck kept them. But he says he throws them away.

"They don't seem awfully damn important to me," he said in the rapid fire, half mumble with which he talks.

"I heard that J.P. Morgan spent a fortune for three of Shelley's hairs. Ridiculous. If he had lived when Shelley did, he probably wouldn't have read a line of his poetry."

Hailed as a social reformer when *Grapes of Wrath* appeared in 1940, Steinbeck feels he has grown both more intense and more mature with the years.

"Everything in life is colored by your personality," he observed, "but as you mature you become more aware of outside things, less concerned about yourself.

"There's nothing that cleans up like dying. If you stick around too long, they get tired of you. Sometimes I think I've stuck around too long.

"I may run out of gas, but not out of ideas as ideas have pups. It's when you're not doing anything that you don't have ideas."

Here are a few more sparks from Steinbeck's idea foundry:

"I'm interested in the war of the generations"—he has two sons—"and it is a war. But I'm not sure I want to win. How the hell do I know what kind of world my sons will live in?

"If all we planned for our children took hold, it would be race suicide. It would kill them.

"A book is like a flag. You can starve and burn people—but they won't stand for the burning of books.

"Writers are a little below clowns and a little above trained seals. God help the world if writers ever took control. We'd be much worse than the people now in power.

"It took a million years for man to get used to fire. Now we have a power that makes fire seem silly and we don't know what to do with it.

"My grandmother knew every street in heaven. But no one has any certainties like that anymore.

"This is no prophecy of doom, but a prophecy of change.

"The greatest statements of the future may be made not with words but with mathematic equations. They may be our greatest poetry, our finest music."

Steinbeck Got First Word on TV: Asserts His First Reaction Was One of "Disbelief"

The Associated Press/1962

Distributed by The Associated Press for publication 26 October 1962. Reprinted with permission of The Associated Press.

NEW YORK. John Steinbeck turned on his television set in his home in Sag Harbor, L.I., for details about the Cuban crisis yesterday and learned that he had won the 1962 Nobel Prize of literature.

What was his reaction? "Disbelief," Mr. Steinbeck said.

"Then what happened?" he was asked.

"I had a cup of coffee."

Mr. Steinbeck discussed the award, the Cuban crisis, his favorite authors, the function of authors, how and why he writes, his plans for the future and assorted other topics at a news conference in the office of his publishers, Viking Press.

Mr. Steinbeck sat in front of a map of the world in a room crowded with newsmen. He was neatly dressed in a gray, pin-striped suit, blue tie and blue shirt. He smoked a small cigar and answered at least 100 questions in about an hour.

"How do you feel?" he was asked.

"I feel wrapped and shellacked."

"Of the books you have written, what is your favorite?"

"I have no favorite. Only the one I'm working on."

"Do you plan to go to Sweden to accept the prize?"

"I plan to go over Dec. 10."

"Any comment on the Cuban situation?"

"I've listened to a great many speeches. Everybody seems to be right."

"Could you elaborate?"

"I think we're right."

"How do you go about writing?"

"With a pencil."

"What is the major function of the author in today's society?"

"Criticism, I should think."

A newsman in the rear of the room called out, "Louder please." A cameraman shouted, "Watch the wires." "Look this way, Mr. Steinbeck," someone else said. The questions continued.

"Do you give advice to young writers?"

"No."

"Who are your favorite authors?"

"Faulkner and Hemingway. Hemingway's short stories and nearly everything Faulkner wrote."

"You've been known as a champion of the underdog. Are there more underdogs today?"

"Thirty years ago you could tell an underdog. Today it's a little harder to recognize one."

"What do you mean when you said you felt wrapped and shellacked?"

"Ever see a fish bowl that's going to crack? You wrap it and shellack it. I don't feel very real."

"What happened when you turned on the TV set?"

"I was stunned and happy."

"I'm not clear about wrapped and shellacked. Could you explain?"

"When you've got a cracked fish bowl you wrap it with line and shellack it."

"What was your wife's reaction?"

"She loved it. So did I, frankly."

"What does a writer write for?"

"I don't think I can answer because it's so long since I wondered why."

"Do you really think you deserve the Nobel Prize?"

"That's an interesting question. Frankly, no."

Cutting Loose at 60: John Steinbeck
Michael Ratcliffe/1962

From *The Sunday Times* of London, 16 December 1962, p. 20.
Reprinted by permission of *The Sunday Times*.

To win a Nobel Prize is to carry the imprint of World Citizen upon the brow; a man so honoured is marked for life. He is at once prophet and spokesman, seer and statesman. Some have shied at the strain. Others have taken it in their stride.

'If I want to write a dirty story I'm going to do it,' said Mr. John Steinbeck, who last Monday received the most fiercely criticised Literature prize for some years. 'I refuse to become a Senatorial voice. There is a curious mystique about the Prize, and of course I wanted it, but it has a very bad effect on some people. The best thing I can do now is to forget it. My neighbours back home, they'll soon forget it. First time somebody rapes his neighour's wife, they'll forget it. Not that it happens that often.'

Pressmen in New York, on the day of the award, had asked him if he thought he deserved it. Trapped, he had answered, 'Frankly, no.'

'That was a trick question, like are you still beating your wife. Russell Baker wrote me in a letter "Who gets what he deserves or deserves what he gets?" The whole thing is so unreal. The words were always there and they've not become any better because a committee of seventeen men said they were good. I've worked very hard on my books, and maybe people will look at them a little more closely now to see what I've tried to do there, but I don't think I "deserve" it more than any living writer.'

The voice is rich, the eyes kind but wary. The man has been submitted to a critical battery for many years now, and his whole manner speaks of a controlled tension. Steinbeck is all writer; in no conventional sense a public figure. Of the great American triptiych, Hemingway attracted constant publicity, Faulkner lectured.

Steinbeck does neither. Yet last Monday in Stockholm, at a gathering which at best prescribes formality, the man whose books have been translated into more than thirty languages spoke with spirit and pasion:

'Literature was not promulgated by a pale and emasculated critical priesthood singing their litanies in empty churches, nor is it a game for the cloistered elect, the tin-horn mendicants of low-calorie despair.' It was uncharacteristic, perhaps, but it stirred the air.

'That was the first and last speech of my life, and I didn't fall in love with it. By speaking slowly I made it last about six minutes. It's another profession entirely; it reminds me of the Catholic bishop in Corpus Christi, Texas. Passing a Negro kid in the street he said, "Are you a Catholic, son?" and the child said "Hell no. I'm having enough trouble being a nigger." It calls for another state of mind altogether, you see.'

It is over twenty years since the turtle hauled itself on to the highway, was hit to the other side by a truck, and in righting itself spread three seeds of the wild oat into the dust—an exact and unforgettable image of survival that was one of the first things to commend the *Grapes of Wrath* to a whole generation. The book has always appealed to the young, and is considered by most critics and readers—except those who prefer *Of Mice and Men* (1937)—to be Steinbeck's finest work—full of pitiless anger and compassion. His latest work, *Travels with Charley in Search of America* (1962) has been called trite and sentimental. He had said that he was 'not mad at anything any more.' At sixty, had he gone soft?

'I was nearer thirty then. I am still a nonconformist. If you're a nonconformist at twenty they call you a revolutionary; at seventy, it's individualism. I guess I'll make that in ten years.' Sixty seemed an awkward age, no longer young, not yet the Grand Old Man. Steinbeck did not hesitate.

'It's a magnificent age! I'm acting on the old Aztec law. The Aztecs were a highly disciplined people. They gave the death sentence for all sorts of things—fornication, indignity even—until a man was sixty. Then all the laws were suspended, and he could be as ridiculous as he wanted. I've always wanted to be silly if I felt like it, and now I can. I feel closer in touch with the young today than with older people. I

spent the evening two nights ago with 1,500 students in Stockholm. I
didn't address them; we just argued, they all shouted at each
other—they were stimulating, intelligent and exciting. There was
nothing beat about them; they had none of that small despair.

'And in the States we have a terrific bunch of kids—we might be
moving into a tremendous age, because these kids don't think the
world is coming to an end, and they are acquiring a discipline, too.
The angries became unangry as soon as they became solvent. I think
Catch 22 is one of the best war books ever written, and a lot less of a
fantasy than many people seemed to have thought. We have Philip
Roth, John Updike—a magnificent stylist—James Baldwin, full of
passion and invention, and James Purdy. Kerouac, too, is acquiring a
new discipline and power of observation. And Edward Albee. He is
marvellous. His new play—(*Who's Afraid of Virginia Woolf?*) it lights
up the stage. I can't pick holes in it. It works. Then there are Jack
Richardson (*Lorenzo and the Prodigal*), Jack Gelber, and Robert
Lowell among the poets. I'm so pleased with these people, because
their interest is vital and hopeful.'

Steinbeck has written plays, novels, short stories, satire, works of
travel and ecology and a film script (*Viva Zapata!*). Such eclecticism
has won him few friends in high critical circles. He has been engaged
for several years on a massive Arthurian saga ('I don't like to talk
about it, as when I do I put it by, but it isn't going to be like T.H. White,
that I do know'). In 1959, he and his third wife, Elaine, lived in
Somerset, under the protective vigilance of the people of Bruton,
doing research near the mythic heart of Avalon itself. ('They were
wonderful down there. Threw a blanket round us completely.') His
versatility is surely one of the most astonishing things about him. A
weighty work (*East of Eden*) may create the need for a lighter one
(*Sweet Thursday*).

'In a way it's like show business. The next turn should be
tap-dancing or seals blowing horns. It's instinctive. I have been rather
dismally criticised for this by people who would take it for granted in
the theatre. I myself don't find funny things any less real than serious
things, yet I carry nothing consciously over from one book to another.
A book is finished; it dies. It's a real death. I couldn't go back. Reviews
come after the event—too late to be of any use to me. Critics like to

know what they're about to read, but I refuse to be predictable. I am not a monolith.

'It has gone so far that a reference to my "jug ears" passes for criticism. I do have jug ears, but I wouldn't refer to the ferret-faced editor (which this one was) so why should they? I particularly deplore the criticism that tries to be traffic direction, and critics who keep their position by referring to little-known philosophers in a foreign language.

'What I was trying to say on Monday was that literature grows out of people, not out of criticism. I enjoy reading good notices, and by that I don't just mean the nice ones. I have been deeply insulted by the favourable notice of a man who didn't know what he was talking about. That is the worst kind of all.'

Steinbeck is, above all, a great storyteller and a great reporter.

'The storyteller is as old as time . . . whereas the novel hasn't been around for very long, and there's no reason to think it will be around all that much longer. A story is a parable; putting in terms of human action the morals—the immorals—that society needs at the time. Everyone leaves the bullfight a little braver because one man stood up to a bull. Isaiah wrote to meet the needs of his people, to inspire them. It is a meeting of needs.'

What kind of needs?

'Needs of beauty, courage, reform—sometimes just pure pride. Here, after the Battle of Britain, you felt an enormous exhilaration. You celebrated the fact that you were able to do it all. I see nothing wrong with that. Homer did it. One of the most moving passages in all ancient literature comes when Hector faces Achilles, turns and runs. It is an admission of cowardice, and it is of great comfort, for it has happened to every man.'

The great panjandrum from Salinas (Calif.), looking oddly Turkish in the Paisley-patterned morning, uses the Dorchester as a London home. ('We know which drawer squeaks. They know my clothes—and in many cases deplore them.') He and his wife have a New York apartment on Seventy-second Street, from which they are shortly moving (too many stairs) and a house at Sag Harbor, Long Island. ('The people live there all year round. After summer the birds come back. Ospreys, great blue herons, the ducks that sleep on our lawn. And the Bay freezes over.')

A man who enjoys writing as much as ever, Steinbeck spoke of discipline.

'I have to sit down at my desk and stay there until a certain number of words are written. When it starts it's pure hell. I've never understood this: we know it's going to be wonderful once we start, but we fight it so dreadfully.'

The chronicler of the Monterey peninsula deplores the standardisation of post-war America, the decline of regional character.

Had he noticed it here?

'You very rarely hear true Somerset now, except among the old people, though I think Lancashire is holding out. My favourite English is the clean English of Carlisle and the Border country. Clear-cut, original and uninfluenced by the Germans.'

The mechanics of survival and the fortitude of men lie at the heart of almost everything Steinbeck has ever written and in this sense he is as germane to this generation as he was to that of the Oklahoma Dust Bowl. He seemed surprised to discover this consistency.

'Is there a pattern? I suppose there must be, but I cannot see it myself. There aren't likely to be any surprises from me now. I think my cards are down, but I continue to have great fun. I can remember wanting to be beautiful. When I gave that up, it was a great relief.'

A Talk with John Steinbeck
Caskie Stinnett/1963

From *Back to Abnormal* (New York: Bernard Geis Associates, 1963), pp. 92-96. Reprinted with permission of the author.

John Steinbeck, whose novel *Sweet Thursday* had been made into a Rodgers and Hammerstein musical, agreed to meet us recently in New Haven, where the show was trying out. We met him at the Schubert Theatre, where a rehearsal had just ended. Steinbeck was standing on the stage when we approached him, surrounded by several actors, production technicians, and Jo Mielziner, who designed the scenery for *Pipe Dream*, the title of the musical.

"Jo," Steinbeck was saying, "those details look good."

"I think so, too," Mielziner replied. "I'm real pleased."

"There's going to be music this afternoon," said a man, standing nearby.

"Wonderful," said Steinbeck.

A few moments later, Steinbeck came over to us and shook hands warmly. "Let's get some lunch," he said. "The Hammersteins are going to join us, if you don't mind. We all eat across the street at Kaysey's. If it weren't for Kaysey's there would be no theater in New Haven."

Seated in the restaurant, Steinbeck ordered a double Scotch and soda, and turned to us. "This venture into the musical theater is a new experience to me," he said. "It's fantastic, the organization that is required. I dramatized *Of Mice and Men*, and I've worked with movies, but this business of staging a musical is unbelievably complicated. I'm enjoying it immensely, and I'm making a pretense of being necessary but I'm not." We asked if the show were interfering with his writing, and we were slightly startled when he replied negatively. "I write all the time," he said. "Writing is a sort of nervous tic with me. I would go crazy if I didn't write. Much of what I write, I throw away. In all of my books, with the exception of *East of Eden*, what is published represents about one-fifth of what I actually wrote.

With *East of Eden* I threw away a great deal more than four-fifths of
the total manuscript. Right now I'm doing a number of short stories,
and a few weeks ago I completed four of them in one week. One of
the four I think is excellent. I have a story in my head now that I've
wanted to write for two years. I've thought about it a lot, and I know it
pretty well, but I've never hit on an approach to it. It will come to me,
and I'll know when I'm ready for it. I suppose it will be a novel,
although I've never been sure exactly what a novel is. Something over
thirty-five thousand words, I guess."

Steinbeck said that he had recently undergone a revolution in his
writing and that nothing he was doing now would bear any
resemblance to his past work. "I'm through with those characters," he
said, pointing toward the theater to indicate the *Cannery Row* and
Sweet Thursday characters that people *Pipe Dreams*, "as well as all of
my old props, and techniques, and styles. I may be making a mistake
but, hell, they can't put you in jail for being wrong. I used to be too
facile. All of my stories now are different, not only different from each
other but different from anything I have done in the past. This is very
exciting for me, and I enjoy writing now more than I ever did. I can't
tell you how satisfying it is to start a new story with no thought of old
styles or old approaches."

We brought Steinbeck around to the subject of a recent magazine
piece on Paris. "This was one of a series I did over a year ago when I
was living in Paris," he said. "I did twenty-five or twenty-six short
pieces for the literary section of Figaro. The idea was ridiculous—an
American writing in English for translation into French a series of
articles about France. I wandered around, asked a lot of questions,
and from my standpoint it was a rich experience. It must have been a
good series for Figaro, too, because the mail response was
fantastically high, and the French people are not letter writers." We
asked Steinbeck if he had written anything since he had been in New
Haven with the show. "Hell, I just got here last night," he replied. "But
I'll probably start tomorrow. Or the next day."
MEANWHILE, BACK AT THE PALACE FLOPHOUSE . . .

Cannery Row, on the Monterey Peninsula of California, was only a
few blocks long, but its inhabitants had a great grasp of human values.
There was the Palace Flophouse, the home of Mack and the boys

who were united by a common dislike of a steady job and a common fondness for a four-month-old whiskey labeled Old Tennessee but called Old Tennis Shoes by its devotees, while across the street was the marine laboratory run by Doc, who played Gregorian music with the blinds down and who loved sick puppies, children, and unhappy souls. It was sixteen years ago that John Steinbeck presented Mack and the boys in a slender volume called *Cannery Row* and it was seven years ago that he returned to the scene in a book called *Sweet Thursday* (naturally the day after Lousy Wednesday). "I can never go back to Cannery Row in a literary sense," Mr. Steinbeck told us the other day over a glass of beer in the study of his home on East Seventy-Second Street. "Those people are dead now, and the place itself has changed. It's full of restaurants and tourist attractions. Doc's laboratory has been turned into a sort of genial drinking club, with electric guitars and all that sort of thing. I've never been in but maybe I should. Come to think of it, Ed Ricketts would have loved it, so what am I beefing about? He was Doc."

We asked Mr. Steinbeck how the Cannery Row books rated in his own estimation among the twenty-five novels and plays he has written, and he promptly disowned any feeling of affection toward any of his work. "The books are a record of the things that happened there and that's all," he said. "I liked the people. It was a crazy place. But I have almost no feeling for a book after it's finished." He drained his glass of beer and filled it again. "I like beer," he said. "Once in Monterey the boys had a birthday party for me. It was a wild and raucous thing that went on for three days and nights. Each man had five gallons of beer to drink. It was the second night, or maybe the third, that Ed Ricketts took a big swig of beer and lay back on the bed and went to sleep. He slept about twenty minutes, certainly no more, then sat up and took another big jolt of beer. He wiped his mouth with satisfaction and announced to us, 'There's nothing like that first taste of beer.'"

A deep-voiced, blue-eyed man with a thick beard and a thinning head of sandy hair, Mr. Steinbeck told us he was a rapid writer but that he invested tremendous amounts of time in preparation. "I wrote *The Grapes of Wrath* in one hundred days," he said, "but many years of preparation preceded it. I take a hell of a long time to get started.

The actual writing is the last process. The first draft of my latest book, *The Winter of Our Discontent*, was completed between March 15 and July 10 last year, but the preparation, false starts, and waste motion took two and a half years. I have taken as much as six years to prepare a book for writing. There is such a delirium of effort in the production of a book; it's like childbirth. And, like childbirth, one forgets the pains immediately so that when you come to write another one you dare to take it up again. Some precious anesthesia sees you through. I've done so much of it now that I really don't know how you do it, and it's not terribly important to me anymore."

At the door, he told us he was leaving in a couple of days for Barbados where he expected to spend at least three weeks. He gazed at the snow piled against the curb in front of his house, and said, "There are grapefruit rinds under that snow that they won't find until July."

Our Man in Helsinki
John Bainbridge/1963

From *The New Yorker*, 9 November 1963, pp. 43-45. Reprinted by permission; copyright © 1963 The New Yorker Magazine, Inc.

It has taken us quite a while to catch up with John Steinbeck to congratulate him on winning the Nobel Prize, but the mission was at last accomplished one recent afternoon, when we encountered him in the lobby of the Palace Hotel, in Helsinki, as he was rounding out the third day of a projected nine-week tour of Finland, Russia, Poland, Austria, Hungary, Czechoslovakia, and Germany, undertaken in the interests of the State Department's Cultural Exchange Program.

"Sending me on a cultural tour makes as much sense as a bank advertising that Willie Sutton is one of its cashiers," Mr. Steinbeck said, in a deep, gravelly voice, and smiled broadly as two United States Information Service aides, who were accompanying him, smiled narrowly. "Jayne Mansfield is also in town," he continued. "She's helping judge the Miss Scandinavia contest. You see, we're both spreading culture."

At this point, one of the aides reminded Mr. Steinbeck that the American Ambassador, Carl Rowan, was waiting for him at the Embassy. The Ambassador and Mr. Steinbeck, we learned, were to pay a call together on F.E. Silanpää, the only Finn who has won the Nobel Prize for Literature.

"I'm taking him a bottle of brandy," Mr. Steinbeck said. "It's the cultural thing to do." Afterward, he continued, he was scheduled to meet a group of university students and then return to the hotel for a couple of hours before going out again, this time to dine with a group of local writers. "I'll be back in my room about five," he said. "My wife's with me. Come on up, and we'll have some Embassy whiskey."

We thanked him and said we would.

When we arrived at the Steinbecks' suite, which was on the ninth floor and had a magnificent view of the harbor, we were greeted by Mrs. Steinbeck, an attractive, vivacious woman, who told us that her husband had called to say he would be a few minutes late. "The session at the university lasted longer than had been planned," she explained, and invited us in. "Everything seems to take longer than planned," she continued. "John has been busy almost every minute since he stepped off the plane, but I think he's enjoying it, and the reception has been just wonderful." She showed us a batch of newspaper clippings about the visit, one of which was illustrated with a photograph of Mr. Steinbeck wearing a black patch over his left eye. "He had an operation for a detached retina on that eye a few months ago, and he had to protect it from the television lights," Mrs. Steinbeck said.

Presently, there was a vigorous knock on the door, and Mr. Steinbeck walked in. He was dressed, as he had been earlier, in a brown suit with a prominent black stripe, a white shirt, and a bright-green tie, and in the lapel of his jacket we noticed what appeared to be a gold ribbon, which we took to signify a decoration. Confessing our ignorance, we asked if that was what Nobel Prize winners are entitled to wear.

"Oh, no," Mr. S. replied, raising his eyebrows in mock astonishment. "I asked about that in Stockholm, and they told me there's no need for such a thing, because everybody knows." He smiled. "May I tell you what this is in my buttonhole?" he continued. "It is a piece of wrapping string from Bonwit Teller. Nobody has ever asked me before what it represents. All it represents is my revolt against decorations."

Mrs. Steinbeck asked her husband how the afternoon had gone.

"Fine—tiring but fine," he replied. "Mr. Sillanpää must be seventy-five, but he's lively as all hell and full of stories. The students were great. Oh, brother, have they read! They asked me things about my books that I'd forgotten years ago. It keeps you on your toes, and it's rewarding, but it's also pretty rugged. I had a recording session at nine-thirty this morning, and I've been going ever since without stopping. For about five years, I refused to make a tour like this, but finally I gave in to the pressure. It came from a source that in our country I suppose we would consider an order. So I accepted, and said I'd do what I could, but I find I get very tired. The thing is I have no experience at this. I have never lectured. I have never talked to groups of people. The result is I have no ability to hold back any energy. We've been here three days, and it seems like three months."

After Mrs. Steinbeck had mixed a drink for her husband and us, and he had settled back in an easy chair, we asked if he would mind recalling for our benefit the circumstances in which he received the news of his winning the Nobel Prize.

"Not at all," he replied. "Only trouble is that I don't remember too much. I really don't. But my wife does."

"We were in Sag Harbor," Mrs. Steinbeck said. "We have a tiny little cottage out there. I had started to make breakfast and was frying some bacon. It was shortly after eight o'clock. The Cuban crisis was at fever pitch, and John came in and said, 'Let's see if the world's still turning.' He switched on the television, which we normally never do in the morning, and the very first words we heard were 'This morning it was announced in Stockholm that John Steinbeck has been awarded the Nobel Prize.'"

"You know what she did?" Mr. Steinbeck said. "She was so excited she put the pan full of frying bacon into the refrigerator."

"I think it was the most exciting morning of our lives," Mrs. S. continued. "The phone started ringing wildly—newspapers and friends. John won't talk on the phone if he can avoid it, so I answered it, and I didn't find out until later that all I kept saying was 'Please hang up, so we can call our children.' When I got a free line, I put in a call to one of our sons, who was in school in Maine, and when a woman there answered, I said, 'May I speak to my son?' and she said, 'Why, of course not. He's in class.' I said, 'Well, that's all right. Would you please send somebody over and tell him his father has just won the Nobel Prize.' She let out a whoop. Then John's publisher called and said John had better have a press conference."

"By that time, we realized that it meant mounting machine guns on the border of the property or going in to town and getting it over with," Mr. Steinbeck said. "So we drove in, and I promptly got into trouble, because I mumbled. My voice sounds like a cement mixer, and in addition I mumble. They asked how I felt, and I said, 'Wrapped and shellacked.' That caused a great controversy. They didn't understand. Somebody said, 'What does it have to do with?' I said

'Well, you know, when you're repairing a fishing rod, you wrap it and shellac it, but I'm using the term in a different sense.'"

"It was utterly meaningless, and only John enjoyed it," Mrs. Steinbeck said.

"I enjoyed it thoroughly," he said, "because everybody interpreted it differently, and all I was doing was having a little fun."

"That evening, we went to a very small private victory party given by John's literary agent, Elizabeth Otis, of McIntosh & Otis," Mrs. Steinbeck said. "She's been his agent for more than thirty years, so she's really family."

"They're the only agents I've even had," Mr. Steinbeck said. "They represented me when I literally didn't have the money for postage. They paid it for me."

"There was just one other guest—John's editor at Viking Press, Pascal Covici, who was the first man ever to publish him," Mrs. Steinbeck continued.

"Not ever," Mr. Steinbeck said. "A lot of people had published me before and gone broke. I once broke three in one year. After that, I began to feel that perhaps I should get out of the field."

"The next morning, we went back to Sag Harbor," Mrs. Steinbeck said, "and in the next five days John and a local girl and I handled a thousand pieces of mail from readers and friends. Before long, the mail was being delivered to us in sacks, and we decided we'd have to go in to town and get more help. Besides, we had to get ready to go to Stockholm. John said, 'I'm going to rent my tails. I'll just be wearing them twice—once standing up and once lying down.' Elizabeth Otis and I rose up in horror, and he finally went to Saks and bought them. I had to buy quite a trousseau for myself, and then we set out for Stockholm and what I think is the most fabulous ceremony in the world."

"I don't remember it," Mr. Steinbeck said. "It's like childbirth, you know. I remember the fanfare with medieval trumpets—that lifts you right out of your seat—and some other things, but I really don't remember very much. The whole thing has become dreamlike. It was so—almost anesthetizing. I liked the idea of the prize, but I didn't really want it, because it's like an epitaph. It has the effect of making people think you're dead. Of course, a lot of critics have thought that about me for years, but I didn't think I was ready to die. I did have some more work I wanted to do. Well, I've been a newspaperman long enough to know that things like this are over very quickly. Before long, people are saying, 'Oh, yes, didn't he win something once?'"

Mr. Steinbeck took a package of cigarillos from a pocket and lighted one. "Speaking of prizes and literary compliments and so forth," he said, "I had a letter a few weeks ago from a bookseller in one of the outlying districts of Denmark who said, 'I feel you ought to know about this. A woman rowed in an open boat over eight miles to bring two chickens to my store to exchange for one of your paperback books.' Just think! Rowing eight miles there and eight miles back—sixteen miles—to make a trade for one of your books! That is what you write for. That is as good a prize as you can get."

London Looks at a Durable Giant

Herbert Kretzmer/1965

From *The New York World Telegram and Sun* 25 January 1965.

LONDON—Six-foot tall, rock-solid, he seemed to fill the room. There is a kind of giant-ness about him. He radiates a sense of vastness.

He lit a cheroot, poured a shot of whiskey, crinkled his Pacific-blue eyes. John Steinbeck, toughest and most durable of American writers, had come to London.

Public curiosity about Steinbeck has been strong and consistent ever since he won the Pulitzer Prize with his mammoth best-seller, *The Grapes of Wrath*, in 1940. But elusive John Steinbeck has done little or nothing to satisfy the inquisitive.

"It is not that I abhor publicity," he said in a voice that seemed to rumble up from some deep, echo-haunted catacomb. "I see no point in it.

"The business of being a celebrity has no reference to the thing I am interested in. And that is my work.

"I know no sadder people than those who believe their own publicity. I still have my own vanities, but they have changed their face."

Steinbeck punctuated his comments with a smile that was sudden and charming. "Also," he went on, "it's nobody's damn business how I live."

John Steinbeck is 63 and the winner of the 1962 Nobel Prize for Literature. But he insisted: "I do not believe that age produces either knowledge or wisdom.

"I wish to God I knew as much about writing as I did when I was 19. I was absolutely certain about most things then. Also, I suspect, more accurate.

"I have lived too long," Steinbeck decided.

"Preferably a writer should die at about 28. Then he has a chance of being discovered. If he lives much longer he can only be revalued. I prefer discovery."

John Steinbeck the writer has been revalued all his life. Many literary critics regard him as somehow unfashionable, insist that nothing he has written since has attained the hard excellence of *The Grapes of Wrath*, *Tortilla Flat*, or *Cannery Row*.

Steinbeck, however, is not unduly fretsome. He said: "Literary critics really write about themselves. A critic is interested in his own work, his own career, and properly so.

"I don't care what is SAID about my books. I do care, however, what is THOUGHT about them."

He smiled again. The smile became a burst of craggy, infectious laughter.

"I am an ordinary man," he said, "scared and boastful and humble about my books. I love compliments, but I am not thrown by insults.

"Like everyone else in the world I want to be good and strong and virtuous and wise and loved.

"I am a solitary man. Unless a writer is capable of solitude he should leave books alone and go into the theater.

"What some people find in religion a writer may find in his craft . . . a kind of breaking through to glory."

John Steinbeck held up his glass of whisky. "This," he said, "proves I'm on vacation."

He chuckled and rubbed his trimmed greying beard. His beard is the only small thing about him.

"I write because I like to write," he said. "I find joy in the texture and tone and rhythm of words. It is a satisfaction like that which follows good and shared love.

"When I finish a book I have a sense of death. Something that has been alive no longer exists. I feel the same sense of loss when a friend dies.

"I never re-read my books with any satisfaction. That thing between hard covers is a tomb."

Steinbeck stood up. Again he looked like a wind-swept giant. "Actually I am an inch shorter than I was," he said. "You get older, you get shorter. You dip deeper, I guess, into the grave."

He laughed again. Humor bubbled endlessly inside this austere, attractive man.

"Call me up in New York sometime," he suggested. "I'm the only Steinbeck in the book."

Steinbeck Here on Way to Viet

David Butwin/1966

From *The Honolulu Advertiser*, 6 December 1966. Reprinted with
permission of *The Honolulu Advertiser*.

Novelist John Steinbeck—with cane in hand and leather bag on his
back—came to Honolulu for the first time yesterday, eager to write the
next chapter in his long and celebrated literary life.

Though he didn't feel much like talking about it, this chapter will
concern his newest interest—the Vietnam war and the Far East in
general.

Steinbeck, 64, a one-time voice of American social protest who was
best and most widely heard in *Grapes of Wrath*, flew in with his third
wife, Elaine, an attractive woman and an ideal diplomat.

When Steinbeck balked at answering questions, she stepped in to
provide the answers.

"He is difficult to understand," she said. "He just mumbles,
mumbles, mumbles."

At 5:30 p.m. Mrs. Steinbeck led her husband down the ramp of a
Pan American World Airways jet from San Francisco.

Steinbeck wore a blue raincoat over a checked sport coat, blue
shirt and tie. His face was ruddy, and he sported the familiar, now
graying, spade beard and moustache.

On the greeting line were representatives of the Pacific Command,
who said Steinbeck will get a thorough briefing in his three-day visit
here from the Pacific commander, Adm. U.S. Grant Sharp, and other
area commanders.

As Steinbeck waited to pick up his leather bag and other luggage,
he chided inquisitive reporters who wanted to know about his mission
in the Far East.

"I'm selling it, not giving it away," he said.

Steinbeck writes a column for *Newsday* in Long Island, N.Y. The
publisher, Harry Guggenheim, is paying his way.

An old friend of Steinbeck's who was at the airport said the writer has planned for several years to tour the Far East and record his impressions.

"In a recent letter he told me he feels the events of the world are moving more and more in that direction," the friend said.

"He's never shown this interest before. He's never been out this way. I think he just wants to get the answers for himself."

Steinbeck's son—John (Catbird) Jr.—is an Army private first class fighting in Viet Nam, and the older Steinbeck has spoken out in favor of America's position in the war.

"Yes, I'm in favor of it," he said yesterday. "I haven't changed a bit."

Pressed for further comment on his views of the war, he would say only: "I'm not a critic."

At this point, his wife took over.

She said they looked forward to spending Christmas in Viet Nam with John Jr. and probably would rove around the Far East for several months.

While in California they visited Steinbeck's 22-year-old son, Tom, who is an Army private training at Fort Ord.

"John says we must be the only couple with two privates in the Army," Mrs. Steinbeck said.

"I am very proud of them," the writer said, adding with a chuckle: "But let's keep things straight: John's a PFC now."

He seemed to be loosening up. He was asked about *Grapes of Wrath* and whether he still hears complaints from opponents 27 years since it exploded in the literary world.

"Some of them have come around," he said. "They're all rich now.

"They're probably beating the hell out of the people who beat the hell out of them years ago."

Steinbeck perked up even more when he was told that the Russian poet Yevgeny Yevtushenko had been in Honolulu over the weekend.

(Yevtushenko checked out of the Royal Hawaiian where Steinbeck is staying, yesterday afternoon. His whereabouts was not known. Airlines said his name was not on flight lists to the Mainland.)

The two met in Russia three years ago when Steinbeck was on a tour with the State Department.

Last July in a poem published in Moscow literary newspaper

Yevtushenko criticized Steinbéck for keeping silent on the Vietnam
war and urged him to protest bomb raids on North Vietnam.

Steinbeck wrote a reply in *Newsday* several days later, saying "the
guns would fall silent and our dear sons could come home" if Russia
would persuade North Vietnam to negotiate a truce.

"Is he still here?" Steinbeck asked. "Sure, I'd like to see him. We
were together in New York recently."

Did they bury the hatchet?

"There was never any quarrel, just discussion," he said.

"I tried to get him to go to South Vietnam with me so we could
both check for ourselves. He said he'd like to."

All the while Steinbeck was peering through the rainy evening's
gloom at the piles of baggage. Finally he spotted his worn leather bag,
which looks like a mailman's sack. He tossed it over his shoulder,
refusing an offer by a CinCPac official to carry it.

He walked toward a waiting car, limping slightly, using his
handsome mahogany cane studded with little barbs.

One more question: Does he plan to continue writing novels?

"Oh yes," he said, as though the answer were obvious. "I'll never
stop."

Sensitive Writer in a Man-Shell of Gruffness

Ed Sheehan/1969

From *The San Francisco Examiner & Chronicle*, "This World" section, 26 January 1969. Reprinted by permission of the author.

Steinbeck—strange, the associations. I sit and remember chill October in Vermont. Busting rocks on a road gang in 1937. Hand blisters from a sledgehammer. Trees stark and water cold in a lake. Winter near. A bed in a bunkhouse and a dollar a day. Wondering if I would ever get out to warmth and laughter. Bad years, those. Once my mother, making bread, spilled kerosene on the dough. She baked it anyway because we couldn't afford the waste. And we ate it, tasting kerosene, hating the bread and the time. Steinbeck recorded such things.

Beyond noting the fact of his death an obituary is unnecessary. Such men are reborn every day as new generations discover them. Steinbeck will live long because, like all great artists, he involved himself in the human condition. There was nothing really contemporary about his themes. Times and places were but settings for people that might have moved in any age. His so-called fiction was a vehicle for carrying humanity's chronicle further.

He was a writer of immense sensitivity in a man-shell of gruffness. The quality that distinguishes his work is an enormous compassion. He saw the nobility in a hobo, felt the sadness of seasons and believed that dogs could smile.

He could write of darkness and make you feel it; evoke boyhood moments, lost Aprils, loam scents, sweat smells and sea whispers. His stories captured the loneliness and loveliness of long valleys, and the hungers and heroics of little men.

At his best, he was superb. Certainly, it could not have been easy. He must have known times of despair and anguish, carving the words out. But surely he must have savored joyful moments, too.

Many years ago, impulsively, I wrote to him after reading of the death of Ed Ricketts, the "Doc" of Cannery Row. Doc had always been one of my favorite people—"half Christ, half satyr," by Steinbeck's description . . . it surprised me when Steinbeck answered, saying he appreciated my thoughts and yes, he did miss Ricketts very much and probably always would.

The two had collaborated on a book called *The Sea of Cortez*, a fine account of marine-biology expedition into the Gulf of California. I told him of reading portions of it to an old Hawaiian hermit named Martin with whom I fished far down in Kona, Hawaii. And of Martin's simple comment when I finished. "Chee. That fella talk good story, yeah?"

Steinbeck was pleased by this. He said in the reply: "If I could write only for the Martins of this world, the confusions would fade into nonsense . . . more than anything, I would like to go with you to Kona and sit still and wait for Martin to turn up."

Along came 1962 and he was awarded the Nobel Prize. Several of the better-known critics took shrill exception to the choice and it angered me. Again on impulse, I wrote to him, saying I was pretty sore about it and felt personally insulted. And again he surprised me by answering.

"You say you felt you had got the prize," he wrote. "That's exactly the way I felt when Ernest Hemingway got it. It was completely unreal—a kind of fantasy . . . as for the outraged Mizeners and Kazins—forget it. I wonder, though, whether they realize how completely they describe not me but themselves. I have known for years that criticism describes the critic much more than the thing criticized. That's as it should be. But I don't think they know it.

"I met (blank) recently—a stooped, coyote-eyed man with small hands, fingers like little sausages and soft as those of an old, old lady. He caresses his fingers in his lap as though they were precious and in danger. To shake hands with him is like touching the teats of an old cow. This is only observation. I have only seen and felt hands like that on one other man—Gen. Douglas MacArthur. And he wore gloves in the tropics."

This was the gruff, tough Steinbeck, the onetime laborer and painter's helper, striking out at the ivory tower dissectors. But once it was done, he moved to softer subjects. I had asked that he give his dog, Charley, a pat or two for me.

"You asked me to pat Charley's behind," he wrote in crisp penscratches. "Can't do it. He had a broken hip some years ago and it would hurt him. I only pat him north of the short ribs now . . ."

He visited Honolulu in 1966. A friend had long known him and invited a few of us to drop by and say hello. Steinbeck was in a plaid shirt, chinos and desert boots. I walked up and shook hands and he reached in his pocket.

"I tried to think of a useful gift for your friend down in Kona," he said. "And I brought him this." He handed me one of those Swiss army pocket-knives, the kind with all the extra gadgets. It had been six years since I mentioned Martin but he had remembered. The knife was worn and scarred; obviously it was Steinbeck's own. Probably it had accompanied him on his travels with Charley. Quite likely he had owned it before that. If and when I see Martin again, he will receive a new one. Steinbeck's jackknife will never leave my possession.

The company was good that evening. It was a small group and his wife, Elaine, was with him. You could see a lot of love walked between the two. He told how Adlai Stevenson admired Elaine, telling her once—"Elaine, you can do anything except get me elected."

And she was telling the ladies about Steinbeck's aversion to the telephone. "His own sister will call long distance and he'll say hello and mumble a bit. Then he says 'Hold on. Elaine wants to talk to you,' and hand the phone to me!"

Steinbeck was slim and grizzle-bearded but there was more than a hint left of his younger burliness. He spoke in a low bark, belied by eye twinkles, and the conversation took many turns. He had been suffering back trouble and leaned on a rough-barked blackthorn stick. "I went to get a small arms license," he said, "and the Irish cop captain said I didn't need one with a weapon like this shillelagh."

He was half-Irish but all of him loved the country. "I know a woman who tends bar there and sings songs. And right in the middle of one she'll stop and holler 'blessed art thou among women!' And you know what? She means herself!"

He talked of his writing . . .

"I was afraid to read Hemingway until I was well along. I'm such a parrot, I knew he would influence me . . .

"What will last? Maybe I have a few things that will go a hundred years . . . *Moby Dick*'s first edition took 40 years to sell out . . . some of the finest writing surviving was done by a Chinese named Anon, thousands of years ago . . ."

He had admired Hemingway tremendously. "When his plane went down in Africa and everyone thought he was dead, I was stunned—held a sort of personal wake. Then the sonofabitch comes walking out of the jungle carrying a bunch of bananas and bottle of booze . . .

"Hemingway was terribly worried about immortality. It was a gnawing thing with him."

Steinbeck counted John O'Hara his good friend . . . "he's a reverse snob and I love him. He eats creamed chicken for dinner and works all night. Once I had an eye operation and people sent get-well cards and wanted to do things for me. But O'Hara gave me the greatest gift of all; he came every day and read to me."

William Faulkner? . . . "when people pushed him into a corner he'd say, 'I'm really only a dirt farmer.'"

About critics: "I wrote a letter once to Henry Luce, told him that if any of his guys on Time ever gave me a good review I'd reexamine my work for mediocrity."

The few hours went by like minutes. We all took our leave regretfully, feeling affection for both Steinbecks. Downstairs, in our apartment, I removed a small piece of statuary from its pedestal and replaced it with Steinbeck's knife. My wife smiled, but didn't say anything . . .

There was no more correspondence with him. Then on a visit to Positano in Italy a few months ago I discovered the Steinbecks knew and loved the little village. I sent them a piece I'd written about it and there was a reply from Mrs. Steinbeck a few weeks back:

". . . If only we four could have been there together! If you saw Hunt in Paris perhaps you know that John had a heart attack . . . it was a terrible ordeal for him and the fright of my life for me. We've had a tranquil recuperation period, enjoying the most beautiful Indian summer on record. Tomorrow we move back to the city, as it has grown wintry . . . John has a labored breathing problem and we hope and pray he can find some relief . . . we still think with pleasure of our time in your glorious islands, and we hope our paths cross again soon . . ."

So his last winter came, and it was an appropriate season for him to go.

John Steinbeck: A Lion in Winter

Budd Schulberg/1972

From *The Four Seasons of Success* (Garden City, N.Y.:
Doubleday & Co., 1972), pp. 187-197. Copyright © 1972, 1983
by Budd Schulberg. Reprinted with permission.

"A single best seller can ruin a writer forever."
  —JOHN STEINBECK'S REACTION TO THE 150,000 HARD-COVER
  SALES OF *Of Mice and Men* (1937)
"It's so much darker when a light goes out than it would have
been if it had never shown."
  —FROM THE CLOSING CHAPTER OF HIS LAST NOVEL, *The
  Winter of Our Discontent* (1961)
"Remember him! Remember him!"
  —ELAINE STEINBECK, TO WELL-WISHERS IMMEDIATELY AFTER
  THE MEMORIAL SERVICE FOR HER HUSBAND (1968)

No overnight volcanic upthrust but a long ranging mountain was John
Steinbeck. When I came to New York four years ago I picked up a
newspaper and saw that my old friend John was in trouble.

Strike One—He was on his back in a hospital bed on the eve of an
operation that sounded as if he was bucking Big C.

Strike Two—One of his sons had been arrested for possession of
drugs. Actually it was marijuana, but from the size of the headlines
one would have thought the lad had been caught with a million bucks
of the heavy stuff: FAMOUS AUTHOR'S SON NABBED ON DOPE
CHARGE!

Strike Three—? Well, Steinbeck was a big man, built for power and,
despite years of literary fame and city living, still a raw-boned country
boy from the ranch lands of Salinas, California. He was a ruddy
outdoorsman, good at growing things, fixing engines, handling boats.
He looked like a clean-up batter, a grizzled, bearded, sixty-year-old
Duke Snider. Life had pitched him some pretty good curves, even his
share of spitters, and tried to throw fast balls past him like a celestial
Bob Gibson and hadn't been able to strike him out yet.

I called his wife, Elaine, who confirmed what kind of day he had

had. Reporters hounding him for statements on his son's public embarrassment. John fuming and setting his bulldog jaw, harassed by searing pains of the body and of the spirit. The doctors had already begun to drug him against the crucial morning probe. She didn't know whether or not he would want me to see him in that condition. He was a physical man, furious at having to be in bed. He didn't mind if people saw him gloriously drunk once in a while, but he was as prideful about his physical well-being as he was about his loving care for language. Still, she thought he might like to hear from me and gave me the room number.

A gruff, impatient voice on the other end of the phone said, "Yes? What do you want?" In that tone was a baseball bat waiting to swing at persistent reporters who would invade a man's most private moments to get their story.

I identified myself, said I had just come to and—though it is always an empty question to ask a strong man who is made to lie down—wondered how he was feeling. "Rotten," Steinbeck said. "It's been one hell of a day. Where are you?"

I said I was about ten blocks away and didn't want to disturb him if—

"Hell, come on over."

Twenty minutes later I was walking into one of those depressingly antiseptic single rooms in an enormous, impersonal hospital on Manhattan's East River. There on his back lay the only living male Nobel Prize winner for literature. With his craggy mountain of a face, his powerful chest, his sturdy body, he looked too big for that hospital bed.

I said I had always enjoyed our talks. We had exchanged ideas, travel bits, book notes, gossip over friendly booze at Elia Kazan's parties, in the kitchen of his town house on Seventy-second Street, and other places over a bunch of years.

He grunted, closed his eyes in pain, cussed a little bit and snapped open and shut the blade of a large pocket knife.

"Don't know how much sense I'll make. The medics shoved a lot of pills into me. They're rolling me into surgery first thing in the morning."

He pointed a gnarled finger toward a white metal medicine cabinet. "You'll find some vodka in there. Make yourself a drink."

Glass in hand, I went back to the bedside. "I've brought you the book from the Watts Writers Workshop, John, *From the Ashes*. At the last class James Thomas Jackson and the other writers wanted to autograph it for you."

He picked it up and ran his hand over it. "A book. That's great. I want to read it. When you see 'em thank 'em for me."

The book was no token gift to the most distinguished author in America. Steinbeck had been in direct contact with our Watts Workshop. When he saw *The Angry Voices of Watts* on national television he had taken time to send me a note:

> I was astonished at the quality of the material. Some of it was superb. For one thing I was impressed with the growth of these people. I am so tired of one-note writing, sad homosexuality is not enough as a working tool for a writer. Your writers have learned early that one is not aware enough to scream with pain if one has not had glimpses of ecstasy. And both belong in our craft—else there would be neither.

Our Workshop in Watts—called Douglass House in honor of the ex-slave Frederick Douglass, who became a powerful writer and orator in the abolitionist cause—originally had been supported by contributions from fellow-writers, Harry Golden, James Baldwin, Irving Stone, Paddy Chayevsky . . . Steinbeck's check arrived with a practical suggestion. Instead of my taking so much time writing to hundreds of individuals, apply to the National Foundation for the Arts. He was a member of its council and would put in a recommendation for us at the next meeting.

It had been John Steinbeck's characteristic combination of enthusiasm and practicality that had helped to make Douglass House more than just another fly-by-night creative venture in the ghettos.

Now, with pain and a dread of the unknown he faced in the morning interlacing his comments—at times punctuating them with the disconcerting clicks of the knife he clenched in his hand—he spoke about the Watts phenomenon and black writing in general.

"I tell you something, I know they're angry and feel on the bottom, that they've got nothing because we took it all—but I envy those young writers." To my surprise he reeled off the names of three of four from our Watts anthology. His memory, like his colleague John O'Hara's, always had been prodigious. "They don't have to search for material. They're living it every day. The subject matter is built-in dynamite. There's no luxury quite like having something to say."

He took a deep breath that expanded his chest against the straining sheet. "That's my trouble. I don't think I have anything to say any more. And yet, I'm like an old tailor. Put a needle and thread in my hand and a piece of cloth and I begin to sew. My hands have to keep busy. I have to hold a pencil in my fingers. I need to write some pages every day. When you do something for over thirty years, when you hardly think about anything else but how to put your experiences into the right words, you can't just turn it off and go out and play in the garden. I want to write every day, even if—I don't have anything to say."

Watching John Steinbeck lashing at himself in that frustrating hospital bed, I was reminded of the stag at bay, wounded possibly unto the death, but still with his antlers and refusing to go down.

"John, that's ridiculous. I don't see you often, but every time I do we talk for hours. I don't believe this crap about 'nothing to say.'"

"Go fix yourself another drink," he said. "You've got to drink for both of us. These damn pills." As I made my way to the makeshift bar, he asked, "How do teach that class? I'd like to see it. I'd like to drop in. But I don't think I'll ever get to California again. Salinas is getting too big. Monterey—I hardly recognize it. I wonder if you feel that way about going back to Hollywood. Thomas Wolfe said it for all of us. 'You can't go home again.' I felt pretty low when I tried." He flipped the knife savagely. He always had been a strange amalgam of gentle and violent man.

"Damn it, got myself off the track. I was talking about your class. How do you teach 'em? What can you tell 'em about writing except putting things down honestly, precisely? 'I looked at the dog. The dog looked at me.' You can try fifty different ways, but you'll never be able to say it any better than that."

We talked about writing and what writers we admired and what writers we could live without. John was impatient with the Mandarin writing that is coming back into style, and with homosexual writing, impatient with excessive flourishes and deviation. In the thirties, with *In Dubious Battle* and the epic *Grapes of Wrath*, he had been a darling of the Communists and the social avant garde. Now he had become a curmudgeon to the Now Generation, who called him a warmonger for his stand on Vietnam and an old fogey for his attitude toward marijuana, acid, and speed. We disagreed about the war, but he was articulate on South Vietnam's side of it. He was hoping for peace, always had believed in peace, but there were times when man had to fight. As the Norwegians stood up to the Nazis in *The Moon Is Down*. I didn't think the two wars were analogous. I didn't say it, but I thought in this area John was living in the past.

We half-disagreed about the hippies. He was troubled by their indolence, their self-indulgence, their tendency to do more talking about art than actually to produce any. "This generation that thinks it's so hip could be the real Lost Generation," he said. "The proof will be in what they produce—and what kind of next generation they produce. We thought we had it bad in the thirties. But I've never seen a time when the country was so confused as to where it's headed. The trouble with the young people seems to be, they're trying to swing the wheel around and take off in some opposite direction. But no one was ever able to do that successfully without maps, without charting a course, taking readings, and knowing the next anchorage."

John Steinbeck was a good sailor, a good map reader, a dreamer with practical hands who knew how to moor his boat at Sag Harbor against the impending storm when neighbors were letting theirs swing and crash into each other. A mapless revolution, a chartless voyage offended the Yankee man of action in whom still beat the heart of a poet.

Tacking a little, while urging me to help myself to his white enameled bar, he compared the wandering hippies to the knights of the Middle Ages. John had made a lifelong study of Mallory's *Morte d'Arthur*. With his usual thoroughness he had studied fifteenth-century English so he could read the Arthurian tales in their earliest translation. Fascinated by the material, he had planned a major work on the days of chivalry. And as always he had something of his own, uniquely original, to bring to what might have been either a romantic or an academic subject.

"You know in a lot of ways, Budd, those days are not so different from our own. An old order was on the way out. Something new was in the air, but no one knew exactly what lay ahead. The concept of chivalry was essentially a humanistic idea—going forth to do good deeds. It's no accident that Kennedy's Court was also called Camelot. But aside from the courtiers there were these individual values. And there were the bad knights who only pretended to fight for the chivalric myth but were actually using the thing for their own selfish purposes. Maybe on the street corners today are our own Galahads and Mordreds. But it needed an Arthur, a Round Table, to hold them together and—"

"Hell, John, that could be a fascinating novel. In a strange way, a kind of *Grapes of Wrath* of the Middle Ages. I never thought of the period that way before!"

John worked his teeth together and stuck out his jaw defiantly. The pills were taking effect, and he was fighting them too. "I don't know . . . nothing to say . . . Did you see what the *Times* wrote about me . . . ?" On the medicine table near his bed was an editorial from the gray eminent *New York Times* wondering in print whether John Steinbeck deserved the Nobel Prize.

I tossed it back impatiently. "Who the hell are *they* to judge *you*? Could the pipsqueak who wrote that stupid paragraph ever write *Pastures of Heaven* or *Tortilla Flat*, *The Red Pony*, *The Long Valley*, *Cannery Row*, *East of Eden*, and now *Travels with Charley* . . . ?"

"Charley [his black poodle] helped me a lot on that one," Steinbeck grinned, and then grimaced. "And here's one from the *Post*."

Another editorial, from the *New York Post*, was putting the great writer down for forsaking his old liberalism on Vietnam. The tone was snappish and unforgiving, as only a religiously liberal journal can lecture a prodigal son.

"John, if I were you I'd throw those lousy clippings away. It's like you're running your own anticlipping service. Only saving the put-downs. But they can't take the Pulitzer Prize away from you. Or the Nobel. Or *Grapes of Wrath*. Or two dozen books that make a monument. You'll be remembered in the twenty-first century, when nobody knows the name of the current put-down artist for the *Village Voice.*"

John Steinbeck made a kind of growling sound in his throat and flipped open his blade and made a gesture with it toward his belly. "I don't want to come out of this thing in the morning a goddamn invalid. When I'm not working on a book I've got to be outdoors, working on my boat, growing something, *making* something."

I looked at this big man imprisoned in this small, depressing room oppressed by nagging headlines and notices. It was no accident that his last novel had been entitled *The Winter of Our Discontent* and that the aging protagonist, significantly descended from the sea captains but now subserviently tending a small grocery store, thinks to himself, "Men don't get knocked out, or I mean they can fight against big things. What kills them is erosion. They get nudged into failure."

It seemed incongruous for me to be searching for words to try and nudge a great man, and incidentally a marvelously warm human being, into a sense of his own glorious success.

A young Negro nurse appeared to administer some medicines. "You know it's after midnight," she said. "I wasn't supposed to let you stay so long, but you two were so busy talking together, and Mr. Steinbeck seemed to be enjoying himself—"

Maybe *The New York Times* no longer appreciated John Steinbeck, but clearly this young nurse dug him, not for who he was but what he was.

After midnight! I had been there five-and-a-half hours. And the man who had "nothing to say" had done most of the talking, on a score of provocative subjects. I only wish in this electronic age we both feared that I had been able to tape it for our literary history.

When I got to the main floor all the hospital doors were locked. I phoned my wife from the main reception desk to tell her I seemed to be locked in for the night. Finally a watchman let me out through a basement emergency door.

A few weeks ago I was on my way back to New York again. I told a mutual friend I would call Steinbeck as soon as I arrived. I had heard he was back in that hospital. While I was packing I turned on the TV news and learned that I was never going to see him again.

We arrived in New York the morning of the funeral. It was in a small Episcopalian church in midtown Manhattan. The ceremony took about twenty minutes. Henry Fonda, once the youthful star of the film version of *The Grapes of Wrath*, read a few favorite poems of John's and a relevant passage from *East of Eden*. The small church was half filled. There were a smattering of celebrities, John O'Hara, Frank Loesser, Richard Rodgers . . . Paddy Chayevsky said to me afterward, "I never knew him but I thought as a writer I should stop work for an hour and pay him homage."

But he seemed almost the only one. One might have thought every writer in New York would have turned out, and others from across the country. Of the out-of-towners, I recognized only Joe Bryan III, a gentleman writer from Virginia who is not ashamed of old-fashioned sentiment, not to mention old-fashioned virtues—like loyalty.

In the family room, Elaine Steinbeck embraced the score of friends who had shown up on this bleak Monday afternoon and said, "All I ask is, remember him. Remember him!"

"Remember him!" a European friend of mine said as we joined unconcerned passers-by on Madison Avenue outside the church. "Maybe I should not say this as I am a guest in your country, but if John Steinbeck had been one of ours there would have been a great procession down the Champs Elysées, all the members of the Academy would have marched, yes, and the young artists, too. Like when Camus died. The whole country went into mourning."

"Well, in our country we seem to reserve that kind of funeral for generals and motion-picture producers, and Cosa Nostra executives," I said. A few days earlier the Walter Wanger funeral had been SRO. But, of course, he had been married to Joan Bennett, had lived in a world of movie stars, had taken a potshot at his wife's lover, and had produced *Cleopatra*.

I had made my peace with Walter Wanger. And surely I would not begrudge him his funeral due. But it does seem incongruous that his passing should be marked with more pageantry and attendance than was granted to Steinbeck. But whether our farewell involved thousands of admirers, or merely the few hundred who were there, John Steinbeck was truly a lion in winter. Grizzled, wounded, but unbowed, he stormed forward even to what he feared was a losing battle in the final winter of his discontent.

Index